SCARLET LETTER #2

...beautiful in my worn clothes...

The Transgressions of Love

by Rod Dubey

Canadian Cataloguing in Publication Data
Dubey, Rod
...beautiful in my worn clothes... The Trangressions of Love
.
978-1-895166-10-1
1. Love I. Title. II. Series.

Cover & book design by Greg Thompson

Printed and bound in North America.

First published 2012

Published by Charivari
Toronto
www.charivaripress.com

Acknowledgements

I have made myself beautiful in my worn clothes,
Like a flowering garden in a devastated village.

The above poem, from which the title of this book derives, is a landay (the two-line oral verses of the Pashtun women of Afghanistan). Landays celebrate autonomous love and consensual lovers. They are remarkably brave acts of sedition against an extreme patriarchy that seeks to control love.

The cover sketch is an untitled work by Egon Schiele, whose turn-of-the-century art was revolutionary in its unsentimental and frank depictions of eroticism and sensuality.

I want to thank the following people for their help and encouragement: Mei Shi, Vern Weber and Lennox Wilde.

I particularly wish to thank Daniel Kernohan, my editor at Charivari Press. He provided extensive notes on my original drafts. I have freely used his ideas, suggestions and sometimes his words.

ಬಿ ಆ

1

*When you are old and grey and full of sleep,
And nodding by the fire, take down this book,
And slowly read, and dream of the soft look
Your eyes had once, and of their shadows deep*

Thus begins *When You Are Old*, by William Butler Yeats, with its prosaic syntax and somnambulant cadence. Like a child telling a story, the word 'and' is repeated over and over. And then she did this, and then I did this, and, and, and. It continues in the same vein:

> *How many loved your moments of glad grace,*
> *And loved your beauty with love false or true,*
> *But one man loved the pilgrim soul in you,*
> *And loved the sorrows of your changing face*

But the world of the poem shifts dramatically as the subject bends down beside the fire. It concludes:

> *Murmur, a little sadly, how love fled*
> *And paced upon the mountains overhead*
> *And hid his face amid a crowd of stars.*[1]

We have moved from a tranquil domestic scene to love, personified as a hero or deity, striding across the mountain tops to hide amid his natural element; celestial fire. Only the everyday is left for the old woman once love has gone.

We see a similar melding of the day-to-day with the fantastic in Dylan Thomas's Love In The Asylum, which begins:

> *A stranger has come*
> *To share my room in the house not right in the head,*
> *A girl mad as birds*

It concludes:

> *She sleeps in the narrow trough yet she walks the dust*
> *Yet raves at her will*
> *On the madhouse boards worn thin by my walking tears.*
>
> *And taken by light in her arms at long and dear last*
> *I may without fail*
> *Suffer the first vision that set fire to the stars* [2]

The mad woman in his asylum room, someone of the earth, who "sleeps in the narrow trough," has become light itself. (And such is the nature of love, is it not, this alchemy? What is beautiful is what you love.) The madness of the world as it exists in "the house not right in the head" is shown through contradictions. The narrator "may" experience something that will happen "without fail" and he will "suffer" the most extraordinary pleasure. As in the Yeats' poem, love is celestial fire, and god-like, but here it is the very creator of that fire.

What is love? It is the primal natural power that ignites life. It is a mad hallucination of luna-tics that, through its vision, creates a world where the extraordinary and eternal transgress the everyday.

☙

2

If they ask you 'What are lovers?'
Tell them 'Lovers are
Set against the order
We live outside the law'[3]

WHEN I WAS YOUNG and first heard Peter Blegvad's song, *How Beautiful You Are*, I wondered if it was true, that love is really a challenge to authority. Obviously, people form allegiances that they are more loyal to than the state or any institution, but this does not make love a threat to power I would think, unless there is a direct conflict and they side with love. I thought that Blegvad was expressing a romanticized notion of love because, for it to be seditious, there would have to be something inherently challenging about love or the act of loving to make it so.

In the intervening years I have moved towards thinking that this is indeed the case.

Love cannot be controlled. It will flow wherever it chooses. It is an essential part of our nature and thus inherently free. It has no respect for boundaries that would prohibit love based on age, gender, race, religion, class, politics, or ability. It is individuals striving to be happy and, as such, love is an oppositional power to state and institutional authority. It can be recuperated into something non-threatening, even reactionary, but this doesn't change the fact that originally love was bravely followed despite opposition to it.

George Orwell saw the threat from love to power and the need to control it. In *1984*, Winston Smith is imprisoned and re-educated for his sedition, demonstrated by his relationship with Julia. But his allegiance to Big Brother, which is given in the end, is not enough. The final lines of the novel read: "But it was all right, everything was all right, the struggle was finished. He had won the victory over himself. He loved Big Brother."[4] Winston has overcome himself, his human right to love whom he chooses, and thus lost his freedom.

The idea that love is central to freedom is not simply a literary motif. Harriet Jacobs in her 19th century slave narrative, *Incidents in the Life of a Slave Girl*, tells a similar story. When her self-styled master tried to make the teen his concubine she refused and eventually hid in an attic for 7 years until escaping to the north. Her refusal was about who was to control her body, of course nothing is so basic, but her refusal of the slave-master's power could also be said to be about love; about choosing whom to form relationships with. Love is often tied to its physical expression, and if free to love she would have been physically tied to the young man she loved. (Instead she ended the relationship out of fear for his safety after the slave-master's threats.) "There is something akin to freedom in having a lover who has no control over you, except that which he gains by kindness and attachment,"[5] Jacobs would write.

The autonomy to have a consensual relationship with whoever we love is the ultimate measure of the freedom of a society.* Jacobs' slave-master saw this in her refusal to submit to his sexual demands. The slave-master didn't just seek physical power over her. As long as she loved someone else she would always have been free in some sense. After her fiancé left, she wrote:

> The dream of my girlhood was over. I felt lonely and desolate. Still I was not stripped of all. I still had my good grandmother, and my affectionate brother. When he put his arms round my neck, and looked into my eyes, as if to read there the troubles I dared not tell, I felt that I still had something to love. But even that pleasant emotion was chilled by the reflection that he might be torn from me at any moment, by some sudden freak of my master. If he had known how we loved each other, I think he would have exulted in separating us… I said to myself, 'William must be free. He shall go to the north, and I will follow him.' Many a slave sister has formed the same plans.[6]

---

* For example: Harriet Jacobs was from North Carolina and, while there had 2 children with a white man to whom she was not married. Although slavery was abolished in 1865 with the 13th Amendment it was more than 100 years later before it became legal for whites and blacks to marry each other in North Carolina. Even now, almost 50 years after that, a mixed race relationship can still encounter racial opposition and violence.

Love is to be feared by power because it leads to rebellion.

"Why do slaves love?" asked Jacobs and I think that the answer is, because it is in the human fibre to do so, to exercise this natural power to (re)create the world.

As an undergraduate student I read *Incidents in the Life of a Slave Girl* and Frederick Douglass's *Narrative of the Life of Frederick Douglass, An American Slave*, as part of a course. A fellow student, during a presentation, enthusiastically referred to Douglass as a revolutionary for advocating African-American participation in the political process. Nothing was said of Harriet Jacobs who, after all, spoke only of everyday life and of her lack of control over whom she could love. This was to be expected. Although both Jacobs and Douglass spoke of the need to have power over one's life, it is absorption into political life, solely, that is seen as the legitimate means to affect change.

This is not to argue that there aren't times to engage in the political process, such as the effort to abolish slavery. Both Jacobs and Douglass were abolitionists (and it is worth noting that abolition was dragged out because of the realities of working within a political process, of slavery being tied up with the rights of southern states and their economies) but the implications of Jacobs' story ensures a challenge to authority that absorption into political life, in itself, does not. It is not only opposition to slavery but also a challenge to the power of men over women, of unjust laws, of institutions that control by racism and homophobia, and potentially of state power itself.

The American feminist bell hooks has referred to love as "the fundamental source of power and strength of our freedom struggle."[7] Like Jacobs, hooks gives centrality to love as experienced in day-to-day life.

In her book, *Salvation: Black People and Love*, hooks sees love as what is essential to advance the struggles of the African-American community. We are familiar with this to some extent in the on-going debate about the appropriate type of political action, between the non-violence and love advocated by some civil rights activists, and the anger and violence propounded by some in the cause of black liberation. An advocacy of love doesn't necessarily imply anything less revolutionary than black liberation, even if love may have become associated with working within the existing political framework. At its most basic, love is simply the opposite of racism and hate in that these are based on ignorance, isolation and fear; hate requiring segregation. But for hooks, the significance of love goes beyond the political debate.

In the examples noted above, erotic love, familial love and friendship are alike in being subversive, but bell hooks would add self-love to that list. She sees it as essential in combating the internalization of the views of African Americans imparted by slavery and racial discrimination, and to reject neo-colonialist racist definitions. Love of all sorts is the basis of self-esteem, community, culture and liberation.

In the mid-sixties, (Lorraine) Hansberry told a group of aspiring young black writers that if they wanted to understand the meaning of love, they should talk to black folks and "ask the troubadours who come from those who have loved when all reason pointed to the uselessness and foolhardiness of love." Daringly she stated: "Perhaps we shall be the teachers when it is done. Out of the depths of pain we have thought to be our sole heritage in this world – O, we know about love!" Both (James) Baldwin and Hansberry believed that black identity was forged in triumphant struggle to resist dehumanization, that the choice to love was a necessary dimension of liberation…We cannot effectively resist domination if our efforts to create meaningful, lasting personal and social change are not grounded in a love ethic…Love is profoundly political. Our deepest revolution will come when we understand this truth.[8]

3

THE MODERN UNDERSTANDING OF love in the West was informed by courtly love, particularly of medieval France, which celebrated the illicit and idealized love of a courtier or knight for a significant noblewoman. The transgressive nature of love was clearly evident by admitting of an adoring love for an individual. This type of love was supposed to have been reserved for the love of God, so challenged the church by secularizing adoration. The idealized qualities of goodness and beauty that were previously taught to reside only in God were now recognized as qualities that could be found in another human.

Courtly love was, therefore, an appreciation of sexualized love but this love did not require consummation. It was love that was powerful enough to withstand celibacy if necessary. In fact, the verses of the troubadours celebrated unrequited love as a testament to how extreme a love could be, a love that could drive one towards love sickness or ecstatic visions. Indulging in love was to engage in insanity, obsession and madness, transgressing the line between sickness and health that we have learned is desirable.

Courtly love was defined by longing and suffering that proved one's love. The pain of love came from many sources including the fear of its lack of reciprocation, sexual frustration (although many scholars feel that relationships were consummated, which suggests the rituals of courtly love acted as a cover), and guilt, because of the dark moral environment in which love occurred. In Dante's *Divine Comedy*, the seven deadly sins constituted most of the steps of purgatory, and all were outcomes of non-divine love. There was a special pool in hell reserved for adulterers and others who lusted; the ultimate acts of transgression related to love. Heaven, however, involved Dante's own version of a courtly love story, his love for the recently deceased Beatrice, a woman whom he idealized and had taken great care not to associate with, but to love from afar. In this case, the pilgrim's love for Beatrice, who was all goodness and beauty, leads him, as written by the neo-Platonist Dante, to heaven. The suffering that brings sanctification is here tied to the suffering of courtly love. Dante, an opponent of courtly love, has become our most famous example of it because of his studied and unrequited adoration of Beatrice throughout his life and work.

Love sickness – a physical and mental condition that had been noted and diagnosed since the Greeks and across many cultures – became widespread among the court (so it was symbolic of class, the poor after all needed to focus on work simply to survive). We remain aware of this double-edged sword of love; of its capacity to cripple and overwhelm by its power. Love is associated with depression, sexually transmitted disease, obsession, suicide and death. The modern version of love as pathogenic owes a particular debt to Freud who diagnosed love as the basis of many psychological disorders such as the Oedipus Complex.

The depiction of controlled passion can be a form of artistic eroticism; celibacy as a sexual act. I recall, as a young teen, reading Robert Louis Steven-

THE TRANGRESSIONS OF LOVE

son's story of David and Catriona, two young people forced to flee Scotland and travel together while maintaining a separation because of the norms of the day, despite their feelings for each other. At an age when I was being inundated by blatant sexual imagery for the first time, at every turn, I found the sexual tension in this frustrated passion between two people more transfixing by far.

The sexualized love that was celebrated in the verses of the troubadours was a love for the Lady of the manor (the wife of the Lord) so it was adulterous and, therefore, a further challenge to church authority beyond the secularization of adoring love.

'Any idealization of sexual love,' wrote the great medievalist C.S. Lewis, 'in a society where marriage is purely utilitarian, must begin by being an idealization of adultery.'…What we can claim without cavil is that both the pious worship of the Virgin and the adulterous worship of the lady of the manor were connected to the general rise in the status of women during this period.[9]

Courtly love was, of course, important to aesthetics. Love became the central preoccupation of the arts, which were a vehicle of self-expression about one's feelings of love. Adultery, whatever one makes of it morally, is an act of self-assertion.

The songs of the court gave birth to the possibility of the Romantics and to the romantic cultural productions we have seen since, which celebrate the radical autonomy of lovers. Novels of adultery, from *The Scarlet Letter*, to *Dr. Zhivago*, to *The Unbearable Lightness of Being*, and on and on, are a direct outcome of the artistic changes wrought by the middle ages. It is precisely the forbidden fruit in social relationships that absorbs, particularly in popular culture. The rebellious becomes desirable. This became the essence of the romantic. Someone like the Romantic poet Lord Byron, the very opposite of the stable marriage partner, is romanticized. It is the door darkening seducer and those who are desired by others who are the most appealing. Love is the escape from an arranged marriage, or, for the housewife who reads romance books, as a way of escaping the circumscribed limits to behaviour from being a wife and mother. Byron embodied the life of the Byronic hero and with the publication of his poem of a young man who has lived for pleasure, *Childe Harold's Pilgrimage* (childe being a medieval term for someone about to become a knight), he became the first object of something like Beatlemania with legions of adoring, swooning fans. Byron was notorious for his multiple affairs with married women and other illicit liaisons, "mad, bad and dangerous to know," in the famous words of Lady Caroline Lamb, one of his many married lovers. The

Romantics drew from courtly love, but forever changed its terms by ensuring a sexual consummation of love.

Cahill also writes of the cultural and artistic changes that expressed and influenced the cultural shift of courtly love.[10] Dance became bi-sexual, and thus sensual, and a part of the process of forming relationships with others. Love was an art in itself. The medieval songs of the troubadours were a celebration of the capacity of all of us to love and, through love, of the equality of all. The union of two people, by choice, is an act in defiance against arranged marriage and on behalf of individual autonomy. A truly shared kiss requires freedom and equality.

Set against an historical background of sexual inequality, reciprocal love, generally between a man and a woman, involved them making an equal decision to share a relationship. Although lovers, as subjects, were typically seen as male while women were the objects of love, it still elevated the status of women to divine creatures, in control of relationships and as embodiments of the highest qualities of civilization. Where relationships become a matter of shared individual choice there is a movement towards gender equality.

In a further example of gender transgression, the troubadours were not necessarily male. Female troubadours were known as trobairitz, the first known female composers of Western secular music.

The troubadour tradition was notable not only for the daring of its songs about love, but also for its many vulgar or humourous satires, which were further instances of the challenge to norms in line with the Spanish songs that inspired them. The song of the troubadours originated in Spain with William of Aquitane who took both the form and content of the songs from his knowledge of Middle-Eastern Muslim arts. Meg Bogin, English translator of the trobairitz, wrote that "a body of song of comparable intensity, profanity and eroticism [existed] in Arabic from the second half of the 9th century onwards."[11]

This sexualized love was also tied to morality, leading to a standard of norms of courtly behaviour. At the same time as it was adulterous it was morally ennobling. This challenge to the church's control over morality is one that is contested to this day by religious arguments that try to undo the bonds between sexual love and ethics. Only God, it is argued, can lead us to the highest ideals.

Ascribing causes to the rise of courtly love is a speculative exercise, however it was likely a democratic and ethical response to the rising authority of the church, the imperialistic crusades and to arranged marriage. The Romantic period, many years later, coming on the heels of the French and American revolutions, was an extension of the advocacy of the rights of the individual. It defended the natural world, of which man was a part, following Rousseau ("Man is born free and everywhere he is in chains") in countering the mechanism, uniformity, and supremacy of reason, in the age of the Enlightenment. It was a political, aesthetic and ethical revolution.

No one better articulated the defence of the natural world than William Blake who passionately decried the devastation brought by the industrial revolution.

He witnessed the Industrial Revolution which not only threatened his craft as an engraver but was turning England's green and pleasant land into a polluted desert of dark satanic mills. In the new cities, he saw 'turrets & towers & domes/ Whose smoke destroy'd the pleasant gardens, & whose running kennels/ Chok'd the bright rivers.' To the north, the new factories of England belched smoke and fire and consumed workers.[12]

Blake was a vocal opponent of war, of racial inequality, "The Beast [of the State] & the Whore [of the Church]."[13] He vehemently opposed their moral codes with their prohibitions against joy, sexuality, and natural love. Blake is instructive because we can see that, at their very heart, these eras of contestation were focused on re-envisioning morality and that the valuation of autonomous love was central to this.

As an antinomian and libertarian, (Blake) admires Jesus precisely because he rejected moral principles and broke the ten commandments. Nevertheless, Blake's fundamental values do come through in his writing. They are both simple and sublime, available to every person regardless of wealth or rank or intelligence. Jesus personified what Blake valued most: forgiveness, energy, and creativity.[14]

Walt Whitman Americanized Romanticism and exhibited its central characteristics of ethical, political and social dissent stemming from the valuation of love. He was the "poet of the body" whose work was vilified in his own lifetime for its promiscuous depiction of the sexualized body.

> *Behold, the body includes and is the meaning, the main*
> *concern and includes and is the soul;*
> *Whoever you are, how superb and how divine is your*
> *body, or any part of it!* [15]

His verse collages of the teeming mass of humanity, celebrated the song and beauty of people in their unadorned day-to-day activities. The body was the basis of morality, sympathy, adhesiveness (love), equality and democracy. It was the elemental component of America, corrupted and in need of healing; sold in the North and the South in different ways, and mutilated and amputated in the Civil War. Whitman spoke for all; the slave, the slave-holder, the soldier, the workingman, the prostitute, men, women, children, the healthy and the sick. He pled the defense (in Nelson Algren's phrase). More than anything, the body in Whitman's verse is sensual and the source of overwhelming desire seen intimately in its nakedness.

> *The welcome nearness, the sight of the perfect body,*
> *The swimmer swimming naked in the bath, or mo-*
> *tionless on his back lying and floating,*
> *The female form approaching, I pensive, love-flesh tremulous aching,*
> *The divine list for myself or you or for any one making,*
> *The face, the limbs, the index from head to foot, and what it arouses,*
> *The mystic deliria, the madness amorous, the utter abandonment,*
> *(Hark close and still what I now whisper to you,*
> *I love you, O you entirely possess me,*
> *O that you and I escape from the rest and go utterly off, free and lawless,*
> *Two hawks in the air, two fishes swimming in*
> *the sea not more lawless than we;)* [16]

Whitman took the perspective of daily life, of love as seen in simple contexts, and without restrictions around gender, age, or class.

> *A glimpse, through an interstice caught,*
> *Of a crowd of workmen and drivers in a bar-room, around the stove,*
> *late of a winter night – and I unremark'd seated in a corner,*
> *Of a youth who loves me, and whom I love, silently approaching and*
> *seating himself near, that he may hold me by the hand,*
> *A long while amid the noises of coming and going – of drinking and*
> *oath and smutty jest,*
> *There we two, content, happy in being together, speaking little,*
> *perhaps not a word.* [17]

The 1960's in the West – to cite a recent example of a widespread public valuation of love – can be seen as a response to the rise in alienation and the spectacle; to the dehumanizing explosion of 'needs' and their packaging as commodities. But first and foremost the 60's were an ethical and political revolution in opposition to the Vietnam War and imperialism. This was expressed popularly as 'make love not war.' Accompanying ideas such as 'free love' and the attack on marriage and social convention were in opposition to the ethics of the state, family and church that propagated war and alienation from each other, and the natural world.

The 60's were influenced by the Romantics and their often radical positions on nature, politics, and sexuality. Young people embraced literature whose subversive nature had been stripped bare by the academy (often made up of "headstick boys" who couldn't write but loved to footnote, again quoting Nelson Algren). The young celebrated the body, as Whitman had. Theirs was a backlash against the censorship of the church and the state in the 50's and 60's that attempted to quash free expression, particularly sexual expression and the depiction of the naked body. Depictions took two forms, one being the 'high art' approach of the airbrushed nude that became yet one more commodity, whereas the other approach was that of popular nakedness, expressed in multiple forms, including live theatre and happenings, and characterized by the embrace of sexuality and the natural human body no matter what its shape or appearance. This was a celebration of the natural, of sexual love and actual human experience. Nakedness strips life of pretension, adornment and the purchased fairy tales of pop music where one finds love with a god or goddess.

In 1968, John Lennon and Yoko Ono released an album entitled *Unfinished Music No.1: Two Virgins* with naked photographs of themselves on the front and back cover. John Lennon attributed the furor to the fact that the two were not attractive, rather than to their nakedness. They were naked, not nude. Actions like this album (so-called because the pair were "two innocents, lost in a world gone mad") and their bed-ins in protest over the Vietnam War, made the connections between nakedness as natural and defenselessness, and sexual love and peace.[18]

Feminism was another key contributor to the changes of the 1960's (and love was an important consideration of that movement). It attacked the patriarchy that opposed women's rights, financial independence, and women's sexual and reproductive freedom. The world of hyper-masculinization which they challenged was homophobic, advocated violence at home and abroad and was characterized by fears of intimacy, communication and loss of authority.

Despite the fact that some parents took the same ethical position as their children and were opposed to the war, or only criticized draft dodgers because they felt it made their own child in the military more vulnerable, the 60's protest became largely one of young people against their parents' more conservative world. Examples of naturalness, such as boys growing their hair long, took on great symbolism and were greeted as defiance of parental authority, and as anarchistic and traitorous statements.

In some ways the rest of the experience of young people at the time, such as the rejection of inauthentic living (like the fascination with stripping furniture and wearing blue jeans), alternative community experiments, human and civil rights, challenges to institutions of health and education, were all profoundly connected to the idea that love should be central in life and that this would help to expand peace, self-determination, humanism, and connectedness. And all of these areas of contestation posed significant social challenges to the state, family, church and other institutions.

☙

4

THE TRANSGRESSIVE QUALITY OF love is evident in our daily lives. For example, love is a necessary part of growing up. With it we separate from our family and form other primary attachments. Teenage love can rend the fabric of a nuclear family, and the structure of authority within it. It is a change that will forever leave a family altered.

Parents intuitively understand that teenage love is an act of rebellion against them. My mother once told me she said nothing if she objected to a teenage girlfriend for fear her sons would marry the girl to show their independence.

A Christian classmate in high school reacted in the opposite way when he ended a romantic relationship because of his parents' objection to the girl's skin colour. He chose to obey the commandment from the Bible which says: "Honour your father and your mother, that your days may be long upon the land which the Lord thy God givith thee."[19] Such is the attempt by authority to try and corral the rebellion of love, which finds its target independent of familial expectation and direction. You will be cast out of the family and community circle if you disobey. The commandment is a none too thinly veiled threat.

In many cultures, still, the ritual of arranged marriages is meant to initiate a love within the confines of institutional authority, which thusly strengthens these structures. Love, in all its manifestations outside of these confines, challenges patriarchal control. It is treated as a grievous and seditious crime and is punishable, in some cases, even by death. Women fare worse than men in all this. That they are capable of feeling autonomous love and sexual desire threatens the institutional authority of those who would control their lives, and who often see women as nothing more than objects of sale or trade. Among the Pashtun of Afghanistan for example (which I talk about more below) both parties to a non-sanctioned relationship may be killed (but if only one of them is murdered it will always be the woman). Both have challenged the power of the family, but only women are viewed as objects with no rights. So-called 'honour killings' of women are not confined to Muslim countries, nor are they sanctioned by the Koran. They are a cultural manifestation of the power of the family over the rights of the individual, particularly over who members can love. Violence is usually supported by both male and female family members; infractions are seen as family matters and those under threat have no legal recourse.

> Reports submitted to the United Nations Commission on Human Rights show that honor killings have occurred in Bangladesh, Great Britain, Brazil, Ecuador, Egypt, India, Israel, Italy, Jordan, Pakistan, Morocco, Sweden, Turkey, and Uganda. In countries not submitting reports to the UN, the practice was condoned under the rule of the fundamentalist Taliban government in Afghanistan, and has been reported in Iraq and Iran... Honor killings are perpetrated for a wide range of offences. Marital infidelity, pre-marital sex, flirting, or even failing to serve a meal on time can all be perceived as impugning the family honor. Amnesty International has reported on one case in which a husband murdered his wife based on a

dream that she had betrayed him. In Turkey, a young woman's throat was slit in the town square because a love ballad had been dedicated to her over the radio. In a society where most marriages are arranged by fathers and money is often exchanged, a woman's desire to choose her own husband – or to seek a divorce – can be viewed as a major act of defiance that damages the honor of the man who negotiated the deal.[20]

Even rape can lead to the murder of the woman. Hillary Mayell's article, which is quoted above, tells of a 16-year-old 'mentally retarded girl,' raped in Pakistan, who was then put to death by Tribal Council. The community attitudes of blaming the victim are not confined to any part of the world. Western attitudes are often in line with the film, *Town Without Pity*, where the 16-year-old German victim of a gang rape eventually kills herself because of the ridicule of the townsfolk after the defence showed that she had a sexual interest in her boyfriend. This was seen as somehow justifying the attack against her. There is an ingrained worldwide view that women are the cause of 'immorality,' even if perpetrated by a male. Female sexuality and unregulated love is deemed to be morally deviant and unacceptable.

The rebellious quality of teen love gets mythologized for its persistence in the face of imminent punishment; when its strength is such that it resists all opposition. The power of the love, and the passion, overwhelms every other obligation. It is a measure of the shared commitment that a couple will choose to be ostracized and become outcasts rather than relinquish their love. The myth drives young imaginations because it romanticizes what actually happens in their own lives where love for someone outside the family is the first step in the creation of their own life. It is rebellion and freedom from parental control times two. *Romeo and Juliet* defied their parents, their parents' prejudices, and the institutional authority of the family. They died tragically, but theirs' was not a moral lesson for youth about the cost of rebellion, but a lesson for parents about where stupidity and the use of authority leads.

> *Where be these enemies? – Capulet! Montague!*
> *See what a scourge is laid upon your hate,*
> *That heaven finds means to kill your joys with love!*[21]

5

JANE AUSTEN REFLECTS A transitional historical period. Her work points towards the Romantics and to contemporary issues of love. She wrote one chapter in the long, on-going struggle to make the love between two people the basis of relationships, overcoming the institutions which try to control them. In *Pride and Prejudice*, Elizabeth's determination to marry for love challenges the aristocracy and its power by refuting the norm of arranged marriages. It is thus, like *Romeo and Juliet*, a love story which revolves around transgressing institutional authority. However, Austen aligns love with marriage, so does not challenge the idea of an institutional contract for relationships (which reinforces the authority of those same institutions). Austen creates a fairy-tale world of one-and-onlys and happy-ever-afters where marriages for love can still enhance wealth and prestige. She represents what is both radical and reactionary about popular romance.

Near the end of *Pride and Prejudice*, Elizabeth is confronted by Lady Catherine, her love interest's aunt (and representative of the old aristocracy), who wants a promise from Elizabeth that she will never enter into a marriage with her nephew, Mr. Darcy. That would upset the family's plans for an arranged marriage for Darcy to someone (specifically his cousin) of a higher social rank than Elizabeth. Elizabeth counters that she and Mr. Darcy are equals. He is a gentleman and she is a gentleman's daughter. It is a statement of individual rights and equality that underlies her belief that marriage should be between equals and a joint decision based on love (yet accepting class structures).

"You are then resolved to have him?" Lady Catherine says when her attempts to curtail the possibility of a relationship appear futile.

> I have said no such thing. I am only resolved to act in that manner, which will, in my own opinion, constitute my happiness, without reference to you, or to any person so wholly unconnected with me.
> It is well. You refuse, then, to oblige me. You refuse to obey the claims of duty, honour, and gratitude. You are determined to ruin him in the opinion of all his friends, and make him the contempt of the world.[22]

Here is the crux of the matter. "I am only resolved to act in that manner, which will, in my own opinion, constitute my happiness," says Elizabeth. Love is about following the path of happiness. It is in line with the rights of the individual as articulated in the French and American Revolutions. Happiness has come to be equated with love and this challenges "the claims of duty" of a class structure and family authority.

This is the beginning of the problem that has challenged relationships since. The emphasis on individual happiness creates an obligation to the self that can be in conflict with having a relationship with another where we give up a certain degree of separateness when we compromise and share a life. It is love, however, which transgresses the possibility of the rights of the individual becoming only selfish indulgence. For love, we will accept a person's faults and pain, and take them on as our own. Finding a balance between conflicting demands has become the challenge of modern relationships. Austen does not present sources of unhappiness that might arise from love, but creates a fantasy world where love leads to a lifetime of pleasure. She contributes to a new kind of unhappiness in the modern world where we have expectations of our fantasies, of having it all, being fulfilled.

This new freedom requires that the individual develop an ethics towards the other in the face of the decline of the moral code of duty and obligation of the aristocracy. But Austen does not fully take the very radical position of championing individual ethics; even ones based on love. We see in her writing the growth of a feminist sensibility, but with a lingering retention of the codes of the aristocratic world. She wishes to revise these codes, which often lead to an unethical treatment of women, while retaining the language of class. *Sense and Sensibility*,[23] the story of two sisters and the three men in their lives, Austen's other most celebrated work, is primarily about this feminist recasting of the code of the aristocracy. For example, the man who eventually marries Eleanor, the elder sister, is disowned and financially cut off by his family because he lives up to a moral obligation to a woman he'd promised marriage to when he was younger. This man is heroic, whereas the man who jilts the younger sister, whom he loves, because of family obligations and money, is the villain of the piece. The man who marries the younger sister is both a gentleman in terms of class and in the way he treats women, showing that these are not mutually exclusive obligations. The moral code of the gentleman, as reflected in Austen, becomes that of prioritizing the love of a woman over the demands of family and class. This signals a step towards the development of ethics in that it challenges the existing moral code of aristocracy, one that could often be selfish and unkind, with an individual obligation to the other.

Over time, the requirement for individuals to be married has diminished. The marriage sprees in both *Pride and Prejudice* and *Sense and Sensibility* are set off because of the vulnerability of women in an aristocratic system where wealth was passed from male to male. Women had a much poorer chance of being independent and so looked to marriage for security for themselves and their children, and the sacrifice was love and pleasure. (The agenda of 'family values' promoted by conservatives, of course, will often champion the reversal of female equality and independence.)

Austen did not challenge marriage nor condone the illicit quality of courtly love whereas many modern relationships are often an acceptance of, and development of, the core of courtly love. There is an explicit rejection of love as contract and acceptance of the idea that relationships based on love do not require a legal and religious bond. This has certain effects. Without financial and legal ties it is less likely that relationships will be based on financial comfort and family prestige. Relationships will end when love leaves rather than forcing a prolonged unhappiness. People will remain because of an attachment to another and not because of a legal entrapment.

In modern India we see a society moving more and more towards the acceptance of relationships based on love, as was the case in Austen's world, but in a way reflective of the changes wrought over three centuries. According to Sudhir Kakar, the literature of modern India shows that this transition is driven by women, but its ultimate goal is pleasure and love rather than marriage. Marriage has come to be seen, by some, as something that kills love. Some couples only find renewed, mutual love once their marriage has ended. Summarizing a collection of short stories Kakar says:

> The female protagonists are often the more active, driving partners in love…The dream is of a love free of all social restrictions and internalised inhibitions. It is a dream of capturing love's freshness and spontaneity, of becoming one with the beloved while overwhelming all forces that would dampen desire and the urge to merge. The dream is of love unimpeded by the shackles of family obligations and duties toward the old and all the other keeper's of society's traditions. This nostalgia for the freshness of love's original vision is brought strikingly home in two stories by the conceit of a couple encountering each other after their marriage has ended in a divorce and the man-woman recover what has been lost in the mundane routine of marriage and its dream of safety.[24]

6

THE IMPORTANCE OF 'HAPPINESS' in modern relationships should not just be read as simply sexual pleasure, although it is that and perhaps no more so than with young hormonally driven passion. Happiness means much more here than something like the current version of 'free love.' (While the idea of 'free love' is now associated with an attack on monogamy, it originally meant the freedom to love without regard to race, gender, age, class and so on. It is in this sense that 'free love' is at its most radical since it stands for a much broader assertion of individual freedom and the undermining of social institutions beyond monogamy, challenging barriers of race, gender and so on.)

Happiness did, however, become an argument for indulgence. The central importance given to individual happiness further undermined the class structure because it was tied to the beginning of the industrial revolution, the growth of the middle class and the decline of the aristocracy, and its association with the growth of consumerism where happiness is cast as something purchasable.

Adela Pinch notes the importance of shopping at Ford's store in Austen's novel *Emma*. "Historians of shopping have seen the era of Emma as a crucial moment in the development of consumer culture, one in which luxury shopping truly could become, in (Sir Walter) Scott's phrase, 'social habit' – habit that allowed for an everyday sense of a connection to a larger social world."[25]

It was a long development, of course, over 300 years, but the industrial revolution began the process where love itself would become commodified. Philip Slater contends that advertising and popular depictions of love create the appearance of a scarcity of love (and scarcity is the basis for the expansion of economic life) through the idea that there is only one true love for each of us and it is everlasting.

> Romantic love is one scarcity mechanism that deserves special comment. Indeed, its only function and meaning is to transmute that which is plentiful into that which is in short supply...Why is this so? Why is love made into an artificially scarce commodity, like diamonds, or "genuine" pearls (cf. "true" love)? We make things scarce in order to increase their value, which in turn makes people work harder for them. Who would spend their lives working for pleasure that could be obtained any time? Who would work for love, when people give it away? But if we were to make some form of it somehow rare, unattainable, and elusive, and to devalue all other forms, we might conceivably inveigle a few rubes to chase after it.[26]

Turning romantic love into a commodity depends on advantageously exploiting centuries of activism since Austen. The growth of the market follows the same path as progressive social change and transgressive love, leaching on to and exploiting them. Popular cultural depictions of people fulfilling fantasies would not be possible without women's independence and empowerment, and the autonomy to have a consensual relationship with who we love (that has been wrought by hundreds of years of women's activism and the struggle for LGBT rights). Another change that the market has exploited is the freedom of expression resulting from many years of resisting the suppression of literature and art (e.g. the obscenity trials of the works of James Joyce, William Burroughs and many others) which opened up what can be produced and consumed.

As I walk through the local shopping mall I can see the connection that still exists between love and commerce as teens use the place to make connections, to socialize, and to shop for friends and partners. Teens are told through intensive advertising and depictions of love that they will find love if they only purchase just the right products, and that you are something less than complete if you don't bag the perfect partner. They have been inculcated into a world where they shop for what they want. Self-help books break down the qualities of the desirable partner as if he or she was a new car. What features are in this year? Desire can be satisfied by purchasing. The spectacle has appropriated the idea of freedom to itself. Personal freedom, freedom from the dictates of family and community, becomes the freedom to consume what we wish. The mall is promiscuous possibility open to all. It is, for young people, without the restraint of close community or extended family, the centre of a new sort of community conformity (the 'connection to a larger world' noted above), and it retains a remnant of class. To fully participate in this community one needs to be able to make suitable purchases.

Erich Fromm described the modern state of love thusly:

> Our whole culture is based on the appetite for buying, on the idea of a mutually favourable exchange. Modern man's happiness consists in the thrill of looking at the shop windows, and in buying all that he can afford to buy, either for cash or in instalments. He (or she) looks at people in a similar way. For the man an attractive girl – and for the girl an attractive man – are the prizes they are after. "Attractive" usually means a nice package of qualities which are popular and sought after on the personality market…The sense of falling in love develops usually only with regard to such human commodities as are within reach of one's own possibilities for exchange. I am out for a bargain; the object should be desirable from the standpoint of its social value, and at the same time should want me, considering my overt and hidden assets and potentialities. Two persons thus fall in love when they feel they have found the best object available on the market, considering the limitations of their own exchange values.[27]

(It needs to be noted that what boys and girls see as their exchange value can differ by gender. For example, it is still not uncommon for girls to trade sex for love and boys to trade love for sex.)

The choice of partners based on a potential mate's favourable display of certain characteristics is self destructive insofar as finding a relationship with someone who cares about you in return. Youth's own peers can become policemen for consumerism, deciding it is the values preached by the marketplace rather than the feelings of individuals, as revealed by their choice in partners, that matters. It is not that teenagers are doing anything different than they ever have since this category developed as a stage between childhood and adulthood, since people stopped marrying at age 13 or 14, but the sort of conformity they now demand comes from the media. Young lovers escape the control over love from family to replace it with love policed by their circle of friends which ensures a potential partner conforms to a prescribed checklist of ideals. Media productions that define desirable mates in terms of money, clothes, jobs, wealth (think of *Sex and the City* as an example) are anti-love. When they become a mere list of attributes, people are transformed into objects, commodities, and who can genuinely love an object? As Raoul Vaneigem argued in *The Revolution of Everyday Life*, we become sickened by only meeting with objects, relationships become a hollow exchange, mere attempts to stifle the acute awareness that we are really alone.[28] Turning love into a commodity contributed greatly to the expansion of modern alienation.

After relationships are formed, one on-going negative effect of consumerism on relationships is that it undermines a mature attitude of love as something lasting, tied to supportiveness and emotional openness, instead, focusing on youthful passion, anonymity and prescribed traits. Consumerism contributes to a perception of the other as disposable. Happiness becomes equated with continually acquiring something new.

It is the love of an actual person that transgresses the checklists and lets us accept another as they actually are. It makes autonomous love an anarchic force in opposition to the spectacle. The process of partner shopping shifts when one falls in love. When love asserts itself it contests the authority of consumerism. It loses the coldness that would define the behaviour of the shopper where the person is just a compilation of features. Loving someone changes our perception of them and relationships develop with people who are far less than perfect, who may have been rejected when viewed impersonally as a perspective partner.

When I saw the 2010 British movie *Never Let Me Go*, based on the science fiction novel by Kazuo Ishiguro, I puzzled as to why the young protagonists, who loved each other, never fought back, accepting their manipulation and death by those in authority (particularly since an accurate human response should have been at the heart of a film which appears to be a plea to recognize the humanity of all in the face of scientific advancement without ethical oversight). The film didn't ring true to actual relationships, for me, and apparently not for others either. An article in *The Guardian*, sometime later, spoke of the predictable public response, pointing to the question that's so perplexed and annoyed audiences. "If this is a celebration of love, why don't the protagonists assert its power by rebelling against those intent on thwarting it?"[29] All youth who love and face opposition, or who endeavour to adequately express love, are Romeos and Juliets, so the opposite sort of behaviour is puzzling.

☙

7

ELECTRONIC COMMODITIES SHARE COMMON features with other commodities. They are marketed as indispensable and are subject to rapid obsolescence. They are sources of pollution and absorb a great deal of our time, from that spent on wage labour to afford the various costs of technology, to that spent on watching ads and discussing the latest trends. But technology also affects human interaction. With it we can transgress the limits of family, work and neighbourhood to interact and form bonds with people around the world.

In a 1996 interview, Ivan Illich argued that, while something is gained by technology, something is also lost.[30] With the constant presence of a screen between two people who interact, we lose what used to be of primary significance, face-to-face interaction with those in our presence, with all the complexity that brings. In its place we become extensions of the technology that mediates human relations. We interface and communicate rather than have a conversation. Illich argued that technology creates a dependency on objects for human interaction, objects that isolate us, and can be manipulated and programmed. He felt that maintaining face-to-face relationships was an ethical value. Focusing only on a complex, global world left us powerless, dependent on institutions of care, such as schools and hospitals, which had institutionalized values.

I once sat in a Tokyo subway with about 25 teenagers in the same car, all in close proximity to each other, all lovely and of both genders. But not a word was spoken. All 25 had iPod earbuds in their ears, isolated in their own little worlds, oblivious to the human experience passing them by, possibly anxious to get home to log on to Facebook to interact with 'friends.' Without the technology they may not have interacted with each other any more than they did, but the existence of the iPods meant that they had deafened themselves to each other. Daily I pass kids oblivious to the natural world they are passing through. They have made a decision to atomize themselves by their constant consumption of culture with the use of technology. Technology has become a new form of confinement, lacking the sensuality of human contact, the day-to-day contact with another body that Whitman saw as the basis of freedom. Love has always demanded ownership of our own bodies because it is experienced through the body; through touch, look, smell, taste and closeness.

A recent magazine article argued that social media "erects an artificial public simulacra of human contact...Facebook may well depress the emotional engagement and opportunities needed for live relationships, and foster the social atomization it purports to remedy."[31] Rather than technology freeing us from work, many people, because of laptops and cell phones, continue working long into the night, for example, checking and sending work related emails at midnight.

Illich wasn't taking a Luddite response to technology. In his earlier writings he advocated for austerity and called for limits to technology because it destroyed human relationships, expanded wage labour and commodification, and meant a loss of autonomy.

> "Austerity," which says something about people, has also been degraded and has acquired a bitter taste, while for Aristotle or Aquinas it marked the foundation of friendship. In the *Summa Theologica*, II, II, in the 186th question, article 5, Thomas deals with disciplined and creative playfulness. In his third response he defines "austerity" as a virtue which does not exclude all enjoyments, but only those which are distracting from or destructive of personal relatedness. For Thomas "austerity" is a complementary part of a more embracing virtue, which he calls friendship or joyfulness. It is the fruit of an apprehension that things or tools could destroy rather than enhance eutrapelia (or graceful playfulness) in personal relations. [Hugo Rahner, *Man at Play*, New York, 1972.][32]

But there is another side to technology (which the call for limits recognizes, and which can be undertaken by individuals or communities as a matter of choice). What should also be seen as transgressive are the attempts to co-opt technology (although technology still pollutes, requires wage labour etc.). The ability to do home taping, for example, led to the exchange of homemade productions that subverted the world of commodities, attacking it with its own tools, stripping them of their exchange value. Variations of this re-design of commodities continues still. These are valuations of creative friendships and attempting to further them with technology, ignoring physical distance limitations, and refusing to submit them to commercialization.

Technology is also an important new political tool in fostering democratic and convivial social relationships. Raj Patel's, *The Value of Nothing*, includes cyberspace as a terrain of struggle in the restitution of a new commons. It opposes the corporate valuation of profit above all else with values of giving, sharing and empowerment. One example of an advance in this direction that Patel gives is that of free, shared software, which is not only usable, but also adaptable to local needs.[33]

8

MARRIAGE MARKS THE TRANSITION from romantic love to filial love. Couples often have children of their own. Love is creative, above all. The new family more often than not heals the rift with parents and becomes part of a new and larger family. The impetus for this is the protection of children and the new family. It signals an end to the transgression of romantic love.

The family is a source of power. It is the thing of primary importance for most, where children's values and attitudes are shaped, where bonds and alliances begin. There is an attempt to conscript the power of the family by other forms of authority, and these play on the desire for stability and protection. Religion and political movements appeal to filial love and try to shape it to consolidate their own authority. In the United States, 'family values' (as defined by the user of the phrase) with its appeal to something stable and familiar is used to attacks gays, abortion (which represents the loss of patriarchal, religious and political control over life) and individual rights. Business also holds sway over the family for its own ends. In the West, and increasingly everywhere, the family is the primary source of consumerism. What family life should look like is defined by advertising and comes to be built around purchasing cars, homes, clothes, computers etc. and the relationships that perpetuate this life.

To give a non-Western example, in China, the notion of family was colonized to spread Confucianism. Filial piety was a central tenet of Confucianism; respect for family and ancestors. It was a philosophy that was pro-family and tied family to the development of the state and an early bureaucracy based on knowledge rather than class. Filial duty in Chinese culture can be seen in such things as the historic prevalence of ancestor worship, and the resilient expectation that male children will care for their aging parents.

Because of the success of the Chinese merger of family and state, the communist revolution attacked allegiance to the family. Confucianism, as well as the state it was a part of, were the enemy. In some ways the Chinese revolution was transgressive in the same way as romantic love is by virtue of its attack on the family. The state usually affirms family because it is seen as a way of maintaining the status quo and ridding the state of responsibility for old people, but the communist revolution sought to free love from its control by the family, since family was an extension of the old state's authority. Its intention was to overcome class and privilege. It attempted to bring about political change tied to personal change. During the Cultural Revolution families were split up for work and children reported on their parents. Their chief loyalty, they were told, was to the new state and the party. "Slogans such as 'Parents may love me, but not as much as Chairman Mao' were common."[34] In the end, communist approaches such as re-education and self-criticism proved to be regressive, and there was an eventual triumph of ideology over freedom. The attempt to direct love, to love Mao, to love the leader, made China not unlike any other totalitarian state. North Korea, as another example, does not just police people into submission but attempts, through the creation of a cult of personality, to make its citizens love and revere their leader. Autonomous love is the ultimate threat to totalitarianism.

Here's an excerpt from an article on new Chinese art (and love is most often articulated through the arts), speaking about Kunming artist Zhang Xiaogang:

> At his Pace opening, Zhang's new work ventured for the first time into installation and sculpture. Both there and in his painting, it's more personal, but no less marked by authoritarian rule. His project was to paint, from memory, some of the scores of family photos destroyed by the authorities during the Cultural Revolution in the late '60s and early '70s (family pictures were illegal; Zhang's parents were among the many intellectuals taken away for "re-education"). The results – oblique, blank-faced portraits where faces rarely differ – speak of an assault on personal memory and history as much, or more, than the government's goal: To wipe China's slate clean and leave its millennia-old culture behind.[35]

Because of the suppression of the family, it is not surprising that resistance to the communist state would attempt to reclaim familial love. I am not quite ready to dismiss this as simply reactionary (although there is a suggestion from this quote that Zhang's work is an attempt to resurrect the past, which could include the institutional authority of the family). Zhang's paintings seem to be a rejection of the ideological use of love in favour of autonomous love, of personal love, which is connected with our identity. While romantic love is transgressive, familial love is potentially transgressive as well (like all love). Harriet Jacobs, determined to set herself free because of the love for her brother. In the 1960's, cohabitation and the birth of children were not the end of the transgression of love but the continuation of it. The traditional family was rejected by many, as were marriage contracts. Single-parent families and communal child rearing were common. There were more mixed race couples and more open same-sex couples. Many people raising children taught values that challenged those of patriarchy and the status quo and sometimes parents completely avoided the form of institutional care that is known as schooling. The transgressive quality of love can be said to begin in the family where we first experience love as giving and selflessness, which is then extended outward.

In her entertaining polemic in opposition to the institution of marriage, *Against Love,* Laura Kipnis writes of the linkage between marriage and other forms of authority:

> Marriage has long provided a good metaphor for fidelity to the nation... But from the state's point of view, marriage isn't only a good metaphor, it's a public value in its own right, a far better system for maintaining social order than a land of free-floating, unmoored desires. As a bonus it facilitates governmental sorties into citizen's private lives: note that the introduction of marriage licenses was just one of the various new forms of population management that modern statehood ushered into being, from numbering citizens to mandatory education. (Historical footnote: marriages were once private agreements between individuals, usually undertaken as property arrangements. First the church stepped in to claim authority over them, and then the state, in both cases consolidating their own fledgling institutional power by exerting control over what had once been common-law practices.)[36]

Kipnis writes that adultery is a nascent type of revolt against religious and state authority. This has led to laws against it in many states. (In Florida, not only is adultery illegal, but as of 2011, so is co-habitation without marriage.[37]) Adultery, in Kipnis's view, induces an appropriate fear from social conservatives lest it could lead to more widespread examples of antisocial behaviour. She notes that the state intercedes in divorce more than in any other sort of contract termination.

It should be noted that social conservatives do not just come from the political right. For example, radical feminists, such as Andrea Dworkin and

Catharine MacKinnon, who attempt to suppress porn are essentially no different than other social conservatives in their desire to police sexual transgression. Their broad definition of porn as representations that objectify women by the display of their body parts "would outlaw much art and literature, as their many feminist critics recognized at the time and continue to recognize now."[38]

> Sexually explicit imagery, often where women (and men) seemed to be reduced to their body parts, was increasingly used by minority groups as a way of insisting that their human sexual rights not be thrown in with the very different issues of sexual slavery, prostitution, and hardcore pornography, as Dworkin and MacKinnon's definition tended to do.[39]

Kipnis also writes that we have come to see the characteristics of marriage (as she defines it; as work and imprisonment) as immutable and fixed. This is part of its power to maintain control. In the past, the generally accepted view was that the institution of marriage was reformable and discussion about this was commonplace.

9

IMAGINATION. LOVE RELIES ON fantasies, dreams and memories. "Love is by remembrance," as Nelson Algren says.[40] We build monuments, internal as well as external. Love grows in reflection. Imagination can build illusions, at times, but it is also through imaginative creativity that the most subjective truths about ourselves are revealed. Love thusly causes the most authentic intimacy between two people. Love reveals "the imaginative qualities of actual things" in William Carlos Williams' famous phrase, seeing things that are actual but only apparent because love causes us to bring our imagination into play and look closely at another person. This isn't attributing fictional characteristics to people but, through love, seeing their beauty, appreciating their good qualities and humanity, understanding their background, fantasies and motivations, forgiving their foibles, recognizing the efforts they make and so on. Creativity is bound up with the ability to love, through which people at their most naked are revealed to us and through our imaginative faculties are seen more completely.

Love is an act of art. A model of what art should be...could be in a changed society where art is lived and not for sale, whether it be something long lasting or perhaps fleeting, to bring happiness but be washed away like a child's sidewalk chalk drawing. When love is reciprocal, two people reveal each to the other through their mutual appreciation and jointly create something new. I give you as a gift to you. It is a ritual of naming and identity.

In a letter to a friend, photographer Ansel Adams wrote about a sudden realization of how love and art are connected:

> Dear Cedric. A strange thing happened to me today. I saw a big thundercloud move down over Half Dome, and it was so big and clear and brilliant that it made me see many things that were drifting around inside of me; things that relate to those who are loved and those who are real friends. For the first time I know what love is; what friends are; and what art should be. Love is a seeking for a way of life; the way that cannot be followed alone; the resonance of all spiritual and physical things...Friendship is another form of love - more passive perhaps, but full of the transmitting and acceptances of things like thunderclouds and grass and the clean granite of reality. Art is both love and friendship and understanding: the desire to give. It is not charity, which is the giving of things. It is more than kindness, which is the giving of self. It is both the taking and giving of beauty, the turning out to the light of the inner folds of the awareness of the spirit. It is a recreation on another plane of the realities of the world; the tragic and wonderful realities of earth and men, and of all the interrelations of these. Ansel.[41]

"It was in love I was created and in love is how I hope I'll die" (Paolo Nutini *Coming Up Easy*) goes the pop song.[42] It is the most banal sort of truth. Many of us are here because of an act of love. Love creates the world.

At the day-to-day level, love can lead us to change our outward circumstances, to find and decorate a new place to live, and create children. It is this creative quality of love, that it seeks to re-shape the world for its sake and to create happiness, which makes love radical and potentially seditious. It does not accept the status quo.

So tightly are love and creativity bound together that the Muses, those children of the gods that inspire creation, are associated with an object of love. "A Muse-poet falls in love, absolutely, and his true love is for him the embodiment of the Muse..." (poet, Robert Graves).[43] Human lovers took on qualities once ascribed only to gods (or at least human females did, as consolation I suppose for the lack of the same artistic freedom that human males had). The young person in love is still inspired to write poems and songs, perhaps for the first time. We are all poets when in love whether we choose to take such a formal approach or not.

Many intentionally create as a gift of love. A child who does a drawing will inevitably hand it over and say, "This is for you." Art, it is understood, is a gift because it reflects a personal revelation of ourselves.

Love is an act of art but the inverse is also true: art is an act of love. I suspect it is for others that most of us create. I don't think that I have ever written anything without having some friend or other, the reader, in mind (else why communicate?). And I have heard others say the same. It is commodification, creating for some nameless entity for money that bastardizes creation. Love is mutual and transitive. We create for each other and ourselves. Art is both taking and giving, as Ansel Adams noted. It is taking what is given in love, transforming it and passing it on to others as an act of love. It moves from the model of love received at home, where it is bestowed as a gift, selfless, to become the love that we extend to others, eventually beyond our closed world.

The transgressive quality of love is also the transgressive quality of art. It does not accept the status quo. In the mid 19th century, Dante Gabriel Rossetti, William Holman Hunt and John Everett Millais formed the Pre-Raphaelite Brotherhood, a nascent avant-garde. In their personal lives they challenged sexual mores while incorporating elements of Romanticism into their art. Although these qualities were somewhat subdued because of the Victorian time period, their work was frequently characterized by sensuality, empathy for the poor and an advocacy of women's rights (several notable women artists would later become associated with the movement). The Pre-Raphaelites marked the transition from Romanticism to the avant-garde. From that time till now, the avant-garde has always been characterized by radical views of love and sex.

"All stories are love stories," begins Robert McLiam Wilson's *Eureka Street*.[44] Wilson's opening statement is never elaborated on, but it implies that creativity is always bound up with love. Most literary works feature a love story but all literature could be said to be love stories for other reasons. Because they are part of intimate communication, literary compositions are love letters and all contemporary literature flows from a freedom made possible by love. The themes and preoccupations of literature have their roots in previous stories of love (including *Eureka Street*). We pursue literature because of our central passion for love; for our fascinated, obsessive desire to articulate, understand, and feel the subjective experience of love, even through others.

Eureka Street is a novel that tells the overlapping stories of two male friends, a Protestant and a Catholic in Belfast, who discover love with others. One friend is lonely but finally finds a partner while the other meets a woman whom he hates at first but eventually falls in love with. This is, of course, a classic romantic motif; perhaps the romantic motif. Love is surprising and does not follow a plan. There is humour when lovers are also enemies. The story is not transgressive in itself, it merely references those qualities of love, but the story of *Eureka Street* relates to the transgressive history of love nonetheless. It is the story of Beatrice and Benedick in Shakespeare's *Much Ado About Nothing*. Historian of love, Irving Singer, sees *Much Ado About Nothing* as a pivotal point in history where our ideas about love shifted from the courtly to the Romantic; where partners took on real qualities and were not simply idolized. The partners recoil on first encounter but this is because they encounter a real person with flaws. This repulsion is overcome and the person becomes someone loved. In Singer's view, courtly love had a democratizing influence in that it recognized that everyone could love, and not just royalty. These ideas led directly to the radical 19th century Romanticism which followed on the notions of the French Revolution "whose ideas of equality, fraternity, and liberty encouraged people to love whomever they wished without parental interference."[45]

What might diminish as we age is our making art for each other as a shared expression of love, those, generally, sentimental creations that would make us blush if they were exposed to the public eye. These are attempts to honestly reveal ourselves, as clumsy and as unfamiliar as this process might be, and they can have great meaning to the recipient for this reason. It is the slick, dishonest prose of the seducer that is cause for embarrassment.

In an age of commodities, a handful of people and productions create a noise that drowns out all else. Certain forms dominate the market and, thus, guide how people express themselves, particularly if they want to live off their productions. Love is an aesthetic act of creation and like the arts in general, doing is replaced by our becoming spectators and consumers.

It is a testament to the centrality of love and creativity in people's lives that they continue to insist on being active rather than passive consumers and to strive to express themselves in an individual way. Some try and move beyond the impositions of prescribed forms and techniques and understand how it distorts honest expression.

For example, in an unpublished manuscript, musician dk comments on sections of Cornelius Cardew's *Towards an Ethics of Improvisation* (from his *Treatise Handbook*)[46] and together they elaborate on the relationship between technique and the ability to overcome personal repression, and express love in a non-ideological way through art. This suggests a way of politicizing love that is neither pedagogical nor ideological, but through using and proposing artistic choices that enhance the personal freedom to express love.

Elaborate forms and a brilliant technique conceal a basic inhibition, a reluctance to directly express love, a fear of self exposure. (Cardew)

dk: This seems very personal to me. When I was in bands and young I was always very fearful of my lack of expertise showing and gaining expertise was an attempt to precisely hide the emotions involved in playing music. In all those bands the guys are trying to express love but feel that's too sucky and so disguise it in bravado displays of technique or perhaps satanist trappings or gibberish from Tolkein. The ultimate macho shrouding was Rush, the ultimate nerd band, who used Ayn Rand's self-hatred philosophy as a way of avoiding honest expressions of emotion. Hence their massive popularity with boys! Over time, I removed a lot of the inhibitions and allowed the mistakes to remain.

Postulate that the true expression of music consists in emotional surrender and the expression music lover becomes graphically clear and literally true. (Cardew)

dk: It is a kind of "let it stand" idea. What I find sometimes with free improvisers is that they can disguise emotion in technique but the basic impetus of improvisation is emotion. Sometimes love but often anger.

The comments above speak to the difficulties inherent in self-revelation through art, of masking this with technique. I think they are significant in speaking about art as something all of us are capable of, as an important human activity that should not be given over to the spectacle and consumption, but an activity that allows us to explore love directly without mediation or repression; art that is motivated by personal expression and not by hopes of fame and fortune.

10

Wild Nights – Wild Nights!
Were I with thee
Wild Nights should be
Our luxury!

Futile – the Winds –
To a Heart in port –
Done with the Compass –
Done with the Chart!

Rowing in Eden –
Ah, the Sea!
Might I but moor – Tonight –
In Thee! [47]

Emily Dickinson's bedroom was where she fled when company arrived. She lived a cloistered existence, in large part by choice. Yet, in *Wild Nights*, she has written a poem celebrating sexual love. The uninhibited sexuality here is a release from her confined existence and part of an emotional union with another. It celebrates the loss of compass and chart, of a carefully guided existence; the transformative loss of self as symbolized by the casting out in a tiny boat on the sea of wild abandon.

It is this quality of love that the Surrealists explored, seeing erotic love as the opposite of a rational ordered existence, transgressing that line between the rational and irrational to explore desire and love by swimming in the ocean of the subconscious.

With her ending, "Might I but moor – Tonight – In Thee!" she has seemingly taken the role of the male in this image of love as enclosure, which would be meaningless if this were a poem simply about sex (assuming the narrator is female, from the many indications of that in her Master poems). It makes sense only if we are speaking about an emotional mooring. The image of sexual union, of being enjoined with someone, becomes a description of love, of the port one finds when the heart casts itself on the sea.

Casting into the ocean of sexual love can easily cause us to drown, as Shelley discovered. In trying to live Godwin's doctrine of free love, that love is not confined to one person but everywhere, he wants to sing a hymn to Platonic idealism but sinks into the physical and orgasmic when he encounters a real person.[48] In Epipsychidion he would write:

> *The winged words on which my soul would pierce*
> *Into the height of Love's rare Universe,*
> *Are chains of lead around its flight of fire –*
> *I pant, I sink, I tremble, I expire!*[49]

Ann Wroe writes of Shelley's poem that:

> He had meant to show that such love was not an end, but a beginning of man's transformation: the knowing of the self from which true revolution would come. Instead, he stood at the furthest bounds of language on the brink of dissolution. To love was to drown. To love was to burn in ineffable light, 'in morning dew, that in the sunbeam dies.'[50]

Dickinson's *Wild Nights* poem trades on the image of sexuality as wildness but here it is part of a loving relationship. She does not indulge in the usual division which separates sexuality from our 'higher' nature. Of an animality which should cause fear (typically not something a nice 19th century woman would be embracing). She reclaims and re-unifies that wildness with love. "The heart asks pleasure first," she began another poem.[51]

Erotic love is a threat to the state, the church and the family in that it leads to a more primary union, one that is highly pleasurable, with which they cannot compete on its terms. Sexual love transgresses boundaries, not respecting reason, obedience and duty. It is madness and uncontrollable by authority.

Laws and moral sanctions seek to limit sex to procreative sex and to direct love towards the love of God and obedience to authority. Because of our lack of obedience, we have been driven from the Garden of Eden. Love is viewed in an idealistic way but sex is animal and base. The attack on pornography is based on the fear of arousal, of the loss of order. Cover it in brown paper. Our children or wives could see it. Arousal might make them forget their duty. Sex is therefore a moral threat. The werewolf must be killed.

Myths spreading a fear of sexuality, because it unleashes our lower animal nature, occur throughout history. Wolfman mythology is one example. At night we become animals, mad, driven by the desire for flesh. Werewolves are made insane by the full moon. (The moon is personified, usually as female because of its four-week lunar cycle.) The cycle has the ability to transform someone into occasional madness.

Seeing the werewolf as a myth about sex isn't a stretch; wolves and dogs have often been associated with sex. Both are epithets for sexually driven males. *Little Red Riding Hood* was a moral tale to frighten young girls, but as some of these girls grew older it became the basis of a tantalizing fantasy of men overcome by brute instinct at their presence. Both wolves and dogs howl at the moon. With the werewolf myth, however, the wolf is something that must be slain before it kills us. It is a moral tale of prohibition. It trades on the characterization of sex as the primitive impulse contrasted with our more civilized development.

One intriguing historical description of love sickness was described by Rhazes, an Islamic physician (850-923).

> In the early stages, the patient's eyesight would become weak, the tongue would dry up and pustules would grow on it. A dusty substance, and marks like dog bites would appear on the patient's back, calves, and face. If untreated, the person would eventually wander through cemeteries at night and howl like a wolf.[52]

In her poem, Dickinson inverts the idea of what constitutes Edenic bliss, by seeing sexual knowledge as something wonderful. Sexual love is Eden. Being released from the garden is freedom, to float on a sea of pleasure and to moor in the harbour of another.

The same inversion of what constitutes Eden can be found in the poetry of the late Persian poet, Forugh Farrokhzad, who scandalized her contemporaries with frank descriptions of sexual love.

> *Everyone knows,*
> *everyone knows*
> *that you and I have seen the garden*
> *from that cold sullen window*
> *and that we have plucked the apple*
> *from that playful, hard-to-reach branch.*

The poem, *Conquest Of The Garden*, continues:

> *I am not talking about timorous whispering*
> *in the dark.*
> *I am talking about daytime and open windows*
> *and fresh air and a stove in which useless things burn*
> *and land which is fertile*
> *with a different planting*
> *and birth and evolution and pride.*
> *I am talking about our loving hands*
> *which have built across nights a bridge*
> *of the message of perfume*
> *and light and breeze.*
> *Come to the meadow*
> *to the grand meadow*
> *and call me, from behind the breaths*
> *of silk-tasselled acacias*
> *just like the deer calls its mate.*[53]

Farrokhzad's poetry refutes the life of women that is defined by borders. Hers was a rigid world controlled by men, circumscribed by borders that limit who women see, how they dress, where they go, what they do, and how they feel. It is a world of darkness and silence that stifles the sensual. Sexual love in her poetry is a refutation of authority itself. It is a celebration of the natural, of the sensual, of individual freedom, and of happiness. It rejects the idea of sex as only animality or, alternately, embraces our supposed animality. Over and over she uses images of sensual experience such as noise, open windows, perfume, fertile nature, light and water.

Farrokhzad insisted on making her proclamations of love public, as an act of joyful sedition. "Why should I stop? Why?"

sound, sound, only sound,
the sound of the limpid wishes
of water to flow,
the sound of the falling of star light
on the wall of earth's femininity
the sound of the binding of meaning's sperm
and the expansion of the shared mind of love.
sound, sound, sound,
only sound remains.

in the land of dwarfs,
the criteria of comparison
have always traveled in the orbit of zero.
why should I stop?
I obey the four elements;
and the job of drawing up
the constitution of my heart
is not the business
of the local government of the blind.

what is the lengthy whimpering wildness
in animals sexual organs to me?
what to me is the worm's humble movement
In its fleshy vacuum?
the bleeding ancestry of flowers
has committed me to life.
are you familiar with the bleeding
ancestry of the flowers? [54]

In the landays, the two-line oral poems of Afgani Pashtun women, we see the same seditious quality of love, expressed through poetry. But in their culture, love is such a serious act of defiance that it is punishable by death (as the assassination of Sayd Bahodine Majrouh, the eminent Afghani scholar and poet, who collected the landlays, too tragically attests). Love is an act of remarkable daring.

A woman's love is taboo, banned by the prohibition of the honor code of Pashtun life and by religious sentiment. Young people do not have the right to see each other, love each other, or choose each other. Love is a grave mistake, punishable by death. The unruly are killed, in cold blood.⁵⁵

In Pashtun society, girls are treated as objects to be exchanged as part of inter-clan politics. Their feelings matter not at all as they are married, frequently, to old men or children. (Husbands are customarily referred to in the verses as the "little horror.") Landays express love and longing, and also rebellion against husbands through a celebration of the erotic love shared with a secret lover. There is not a single landay celebrating conjugal relationships.

In secret I burn, in secret I weep,
I am the Pashtun woman who can't unveil her love.

Just to see you I invent circuitous walks.
Like a peddler I cry at every door.

Hold me tightly in your arms,
I have prowled around solitude's prison far too long.

Give me your hand, my love, and let us go into the fields
So we can love each other or fall together beneath the blows of knives.

Your love is water and it is fire,
Flames are consuming me, waves are swallowing me up.

God, is this then a sin?
You created the world's garden and the flower that
*really pleases me is the one I took.*⁵⁶

The landays are seditious not only for the fact of love but for the celebration of adultery. It is sedition because marriage is a means of the enforcement of power. The nature of the control defines the form of resistance. Here love must be fleeting and insistent. Sex or sexual love resists dehumanization. Sexual love is a direct challenge to religious power.

I grow crazier with each passing day,
When I pass the tomb of a holy man I throw stones
*at it for all my unrequited wishes.*⁵⁷

What we see in the poetry of the women cited above is a description of love as a loss of self, as an emotional and physical bonding with another marked

The Trangressions of Love

by choice and sensuality, and as an act of daring. Sex is not something separate from love, but a reinforcement and sharing of its qualities.

Not surprisingly, we see similar characteristics being ascribed to love by female mystics and nuns where sexuality is not something apart from, but central to experiencing the ecstasy and union of love. That love of God shares these characteristics is very unsettling to some who see only the sacrilegious aspect of it, that love of God is not unique, that sexuality is a part of our being and a part of how we experience love.

What mystics and nuns describe is a way of experiencing love of God that is in common with the corporeal love directed at another human. In some cases, such as in St Teresa d'Avila's meeting with an angel, religious rapture clearly seems to be a sexual experience. Bernini's depiction of this meeting appears to show an orgasm brought on by the angel. (This is vigorously denied by some, of course, who argue on behalf of idealism, that it is sublime truth so not sordid sexuality).

> I saw in his hand a long spear of gold, and at the iron's point there seemed to be a little fire. He appeared to me to be thrusting it at times into my heart, and to pierce my very entrails; when he drew it out, he seemed to draw them out also, and to leave me all on fire with a great love of God. The pain was so great, that it made me moan; and yet so surpassing was the sweetness of this excessive pain, that I could not wish to be rid of it. The soul is satisfied now with nothing less than God. The pain is not bodily, but spiritual; though the body has its share in it. It is a caressing of love so sweet which now takes place between the soul and God, that I pray God of His goodness to make him experience it who may think that I am lying.[58]

Christianity has it both ways, it co-opts sex at the same time as condemning it. (Christianity always co-opts from other cultures and popular culture to obtain converts. Easter and Christmas, for example, fall at the times of the spring and winter equinoxes and take many of their customs from pagan rituals, co-opting them to appeal to pagans.) In the case of St. Teresa we can refer back to many cases of sexual union between gods and humans that her story seems to copy. Danaë, for example, was raped by Zeus who made a habit of such transgressions, which inevitably led to tragic ends. In St. Teresa's Christianized version of the Zeus myth, the angel's original transgression eventually becomes consensual and pleasurable. It is not surprising, since Christianity repressed women's sensuality, that sexual love would be sublimated. (People refused to follow the limitations of sex as an animal function, so it was grudgingly permitted – such as in Thomas Aquinas's famous dictum that it is better to marry than to burn.) For religious women, overcoming this repression led to sexuality emerging in mystical forms.

Marguerite Porete was a 14th century Beguine who wrote a treatise identifying the characteristics of love. She utilizes erotic imagery and concepts from courtly love to describe the love of God.

> Startling imagery may be accompanied by startling paradox: the soul "swims in the sea of joy," yet "feels no joy since she herself is joy." Striking too is Marguerite's joining of the religious with the courtly-erotic. The soul longs for her far-off beloved just as a princess of legend once longed "to see and to have" Alexander; love tells the soul to express her desire "nakedly."[59]

Porete wrote of a one-to-one communion with the other, in this case with God, that is created by love, by the annihilation of the soul which allows for a harbouring of the other within.

Porete was publicly burned at the stake in central Paris in 1310 (for embracing love!!). The reasons behind this are subject to debate. Simon Critchley has asserted that it was because in saying that it was possible to know God directly, through love, it meant there was no role for the church.[60] She refused to recant her views or acknowledge the authority of the Inquisition. The intention of her views may not have been sedition as such, but this was its effect. Love not only transgresses our own limits, linking us with another, but her writing of this challenged the authority of the church.

In *The Mirror of Simple Souls*, Porete wrote that the soul passes through seven stages to reach spiritual perfection. A person begins with a yearning desire which becomes an ardent desire where love and reason are united in the direction they wish to take. Reason and will are eventually left behind as desirous love becomes divine love. With love, she moves past the day-to-day world of desire and will. She hacks away at her soul to make a space within herself for love to enter. Her annihilated soul has no will of its own and is in a state of nothingness waiting to be filled up by her union with God. She has lost her identity like the water of a river flowing into an ocean.

> At this point the soul in her yearning love despairs that she will ever be able to please her beloved. Her own ardour is pressed to its limits when she ponders the possibilities which will ultimately cause her desire to be annihilated. As if God himself were pressing these hard questions, the soul considers that God might be better pleased if she should love another more than him; that he might love another more than her; that he might will that another might love her more than he.[61]

Finally, her soul is annihilated. She is empty and humble, and God enters. The sixth stage, the union with God, can happen over and over. Critchley wrote:

> What Porete is trying to describe is the transformation of the self through an act of love...(Jacques) Lacan makes an extraordinary remark, as if he were replying to (Norman) Cohn; he says: 'to reduce mysticism to the business of fucking is to miss the point entirely' – and I agree with that... And this is what's interesting: that female mystics are on the path of an experience of the en plus, an experience of transgression that exceeds the order of knowledge. What interests me with the question of love is that dimension of transgression, which Lacan elsewhere identifies with truth. This truth is not a propositional truth, but some sort of ecstatic experience of truth...So love is an act of absolute spiritual daring that eviscerates the old self in order that something new can come into being – and this is what I think is behind this idea – to hew and hack away at oneself in order to make a space that is large enough for love to enter.[62]

In spite of Critchley's denial, Porete seems to me to not only be speaking of love as a spiritual attainment, but to be describing it in a very sexual way. I don't think stripping it of its sexual aspect ennobles what she is saying. Sex is not base. Porete, like the other women mentioned above, seems to be reintegrating sex with love. She begins with desirous love expressed in a physical way and this leads to a complete absorption of the other, physically and spiritually. Sex is what distinguishes this love from that which she feels for 'Mothers' and 'Sisters.' She, like the secular women poets mentioned above, sees love as a loss of self, of harbouring and uniting with the loved one, of being daring. Perhaps the denial of the sexual aspect of Porete's description of love is because it is reminiscent of what has come to be passé in the West – sexual revolution – but in the West and elsewhere it was, and is, a rebellious act for women to claim sexuality as a natural part of themselves. Feminism requires sexual frankness. Modern feminism is a continuation of the medieval proto-feminist rebellion of women like Porete.

What distinguishes Porete from Dickinson and the women poets mentioned above, is that the latter stake a claim to sex with another human. They embrace corporeal pleasure, orgasm, and define sex in their own terms. It is something more than just 'fucking', but that is part of it. It is reclaimed as something nice women may do. The physical act is an integral part of the expression of the act of love. They transgress created boundaries that separate the sublime and base, the idealistic and empirical, rationality and madness, and sex and love.

While Dickinson was an atheist, the other poets mentioned were not (presumably), but they all refuse the Edenic idea of bliss as sin. They embrace the knowledge of sexuality, refusing to see it as sin but as an expression of love, as a secular 'truth,' and they express this through aesthetic creation. The literature of love is a refutation of anti-aesthetic ideas that have been in circulation since Plato, that the arts should be in service to authority. This was an ethical argument. The personal 'imbalance' that the arts create, in exciting happiness and desire, supposedly brought vice and misery. The interest in the illusion created by the arts is an interest in the irrational. It is indulgence and the loss of self-control.

The literature of erotic love is a rejection of Platonic and religious idealism. It is about real people and real pleasures. In a repressive society, sex itself is transgressive. The proliferation of the novel, in particular, is an ongoing aesthetic challenge to anti-aesthetics. Adultery remains a common theme. Sex has been seen as a means of self-realization. Austen's writing and many other cultural productions testify also to our desire to feel the feelings of being loved. For others, fiction indulges the fantasy of being desired sexually.

The state and church in the West have sought to control representations of love, believing that they are performing the function of protecting society; in this case from sexual urges which would rend the social fabric of stability. Policing the forbidden is always cast as being for our own good at the same time as it strengthens power. Sex is seen as disgusting, involving the same organs used to expel waste. When the practice and depiction of sex is called deviancy, its practice becomes a form of subversion and it is policed like all other radical acts. In the US, for example, for 100 years pornography law was implemented by the US Post Office, which decided what was pornography. James Joyce was deemed pornographic as were many other novelists and artists. The actions of authorities, in limiting artistic distribution, could cripple a company (which led to self-censorship). But stopping images of sex was only part of their mandate. They were also charged with finding radical and seditious political material.[63] The different genres are invariably linked.

The populace itself becomes charged with enforcing bigotry and policing the agenda of authority through branding and ostracism. Outing gays, for example, is meant to decorate them with a scarlet letter, much as Hester Prynne in Hawthorne's novel was branded for an act of adultery, with incredible cruelty. Like Hester, standing up to this is an act of bravery that insists on one's freedom to love who one chooses and to express that sexually.

There is a linkage between the control of sexuality and a conservative political agenda. In New Orleans, for instance, a conviction for prostitution may land one on the register of sexual offenders. This leads to stigmatizing individuals and making them the victims of harassment wherever they live. Many people on the register are people who left home, defying parental authority, and turned to prostitution to survive. They are poor, and most often black women. Branding them with a scarlet letter ensures that the community polices the behaviour of their fellow citizens.[64] When most people on the list are there solely for downloading pictures it can be argued that the list is meant for protection and ostracism, not only from those who pose a physical threat, but from those who pose a moral threat to 'family values.'

11

IN HANS CHRISTIAN ANDERSON'S fairy tale, *The Little Mermaid*,[65] a young mermaid, upon reaching the age of 15, gets to look at the world above the surface of the ocean. She watches a handsome prince from afar, falls in love with him and decides to live in his world. For love she will leave the idyllic world of her youth forever. The little mermaid visits a Sea Witch who sells her a potion which gives her beautiful legs, but also robs her of her voice and mermaid identity. The Sea Witch warns the mermaid that in order to gain a soul and have eternal life, the prince must love and marry her. Otherwise she will die a day after the prince marries.

The little mermaid, during the time when first watching the prince, had occasion to rescue him after he was washed overboard during a great storm, but the prince thinks it was another who saved him and he is seduced by that one's beauty. He thusly falls in love with the wrong woman and the little mermaid's love is unrequited. The feet she exchanged her flipper for bleed, and she is in excruciating pain when she walks (a nice metaphor for how we view unrequited love), yet she dances for the prince at court, which delights him.

The story of the little mermaid is offensive to our feminist sensibilities (beyond the more general feminist objections to the reactionary court society of fairy tales with its defined roles for men and women). She is a young woman who loses her voice and identity in a relationship, yet chooses to stay in it. Her legs are there to dance and please the man. She needs this man to love and marry her in order to be fully human. She will die without his love so continues to live a life of self-sacrifice centred around him, although he cannot love her because he has been seduced by the beauty of another.

But the little mermaid did not die. After the prince chose another and the end of the little mermaid's existence is certain, her sisters offer her a knife. If she kills the prince, she can return to her underwater world and thus save herself. The mermaid can't bring herself to do this. When the prince marries, the little mermaid becomes spirit. In exchange for 200 years of good deeds she will gain a soul and eternal life.

The little mermaid's redemption indicates that this is an angel story. It is the fantasy that someone sees our goodness and, in the end, we are rewarded for our deeds. The central themes of this fairy tale are also often the same as those found in stories of angels (as elucidated in Greg Thompson's video, *Angel Day Turning*).[66] E.g. A wish is granted, but it brings pain, and beauty is a form of evil. *The Little Mermaid* is possibly a story of personal consolation for Anderson in the way that *The Ugly Duckling* was said to be. His stories show empathy for those who are unloved or rejected.

The end of the story does not change the fact that the story is still one of sacrifice however. Instead of condemning it, Anderson's story seems to say that this sort of self-sacrifice is ennobling and redemptive (which could be seen as justifications for living a life of drudgery...you will be rewarded in heaven). But there is something more in the ending than rescuing a happy or reactionary resolution. The moral dilemma that the little mermaid must confront – that she can only live by killing the one she loves – is the ethical choice at the heart of love. The other person, their identity and feelings can be sacrificed for our own pleasure. The little mermaid has sacrificed herself for the other and she has refused to sacrifice him in turn. For this she will gain a soul and live with God. She has acquitted herself, in love, with dignity and virtue. The story is thus a moral one. *The Little Mermaid* thus touches on lasting themes about love and selfless, and selfish, sacrifice.

In spite of its other aspects however, the story of the little mermaid is seen as one of unrequited love. It is this which we find unsettling. Unrequited love subverts the expectations of fictional romance. The young lover gives up her family and home for love, yet finds only death. Unrequited love is seldom seen as anything but sad.

We find instances of unrequited love to be heartbreaking. The world is a difficult place. To not be alone, humans reach for one another. To be alone, therefore, carries a certain tragedy to it. Perhaps no more so than for children as they begin to realize their detachment from the world and their families, and feel the fear that this realization entails. In *Memoirs of a Dutiful Daughter*, Simone De Beauvoir wrote of her childhood:

> Andersen taught me what melancholy is; in his tales objects suffer from neglect, are broken and pine away without deserving their unhappy fate; the little mermaid, before she passed into oblivion, was in agony at every step she took, as if she were walking on red-hot cinders, yet she had not done anything wrong: her tortures and her death made me sick at heart.[67]

The Surrealists formulated a different type of objection to unrequited love. *The Little Mermaid* harkens back to stories of courtly love, where monumental love was evidenced by its persistence in the face of indifference. But this sort of persistence is no longer admirable. It is the worst sort of love sickness.

> Surrealist love picks up on the tradition of courtly love, with all its inbred contraries: to possess is no longer to love, so the truest love is in the pursuit itself...But what differentiates the surrealist vision from the courtly love of medieval Provençal poets is the marvellous possibility that an end can be reached, a love consummated, while utilizing desire for that end can be reached, for the consummation, continues.[68]

In *The Art of Loving*, Erich Fromm (who, ironically, preaches the idea of love as giving) appreciatively quotes Marx's comment that, "If...as a loving person you do not make of yourself a loved person, then your love is impotent, a misfortune."[69] Fromm's viewpoint is startling because he seems with this to insist that love be quid pro quo in spite of the fact that his book is a refutation of the tendency of love to become a commercial trade-off. He here appeals to his readers to give love, not for itself, but because their love will be returned; that's the payoff. He is arguing for love as a transaction. I suspect that what motivates Fromm is that he wants to distinguish love as giving from love as sacrifice. That giving is not simply drudgery and anti-feminist. There are political overtones, as well, in views insisting that love must be returned. It is to argue that love should not be either servitude or prostitution, but an act of exchange among equals; a socialist act. It is also perhaps an argument that we break down social barriers that could prevent mutual love, such as two people coming from different social classes. But whatever his motives, love given but not returned is seen as a misfortune.

Philip Slater has argued that stories of tragic and unrequited love contribute to the idea that love is rare, in turn contributing to the development of true love as a commodity. There is some validity in this to the extent that we are told that there is only one true love for each of us. Popular literature does not hold with the idea of Don Juan, that we can love more than one person. The idea that the lack of love's return is a sort of death makes it tragic.

But the reality is that much of the love that we feel is not reciprocated and this is not necessarily political (and while it can be tragic it is more commonly not). Someone simply does not choose to return it. It is selfish and self-serving to demand we receive some satisfaction in return. We must be careful to separate the sad lack of love's return because of social factors from the fact of its non-return by someone else's decision. People gaining the freedom to love who they wish means much love will be unrequited. The possibility of unrequited love is an outcome of people loving freely.

Without unrequited love there would be no love. We learn of love's intensity when it doesn't find a home, of vulnerability, that self-sacrifice will not win love and we learn to appreciate love. We take the risk to love, transgressing the comfort of solitude, and reach out to others. We love without knowing whether it will be returned or not. "No se puede vivir sin amar" (Malcolm Lowry, *Under the Volcano*)[70] We cannot live without loving. I suspect that people continue to love, even after it is not returned because we need to love. It makes us human. Unrequited love is not impotence, but an expression of this humanity. It is like the potlatch; an act of giving and not a financial-like exchange. It is a rejection of the coldness of commodification, the mutual measurement of others and coming to some kind of terms before we move forward with love. Selfless love is central to ethical relations. The selfless love of a mother for a newborn is our first glimpse of love. It is what we learn about love and extend outward.

In one of his Calamus poems, Walt Whitman would write:

> *Sometimes with one I love, I fill myself with rage,*
> *for fear I effuse unreturned love;*
> *But now I think there is no unreturned love – the*
> *pay is certain, one way or another,*

Doubtless I could not have perceived the universe, or written one of my poems, if I had not freely given myself to comrades, to love.[71]

☙

12

KIERKEGAARD STOOD APART FROM the church, but still maintained a Christian approach to ethics.

"You shall love your neighbour as yourself" (Mark 22:39Bible)… Kierkegaard makes a foundational distinction between 'preferential love' and 'commanded love.' The former sort, which includes erotic love (eros) and friendship (philia), is what we commonly call love, where love is evoked by the lovable features that the other bears (or does not)…Preferential love, Kierkegaard says, is 'pagan'…Commanded love, on the other hand, is profoundly egalitarian and non-preferential, and it is directed to the 'neighbour'…That love…is called by still a third Greek word for love: agape.[72]

Christian agape has multiple meanings, but generally refers to the love of God for humanity and, in line with that, the love that humanity is expected to extend to God and each other. Christian charity. "Love your neighbour as yourself." This primary ethical principle, asserting that ethics begins with love, only happens, according to Kierkegaard, with submission to God's command. "You shall…" All love of family and friends is classed as selfishness, pagan love that imparts no ethical obligation. It is only through God's command that we act ethically.

The biblical injunction to love one's neighbour is a significant ethical principle. It imparts an individual obligation to ethically treat all others without distinction based on an application of the love which we know. And this obligation extends beyond our immediate circle. John Caputo says that Kierkegaard does not use the word neighbours in its usual sense; "this word commonly means, those who are nearest and dearest…Rather, he means the 'next one' you meet…hence anyone, everyone."[73]

In his refusal of subservience to the church, Kierkegaard rejects its institutional authority and insists on individual responsibility, which became a central tenet of existentialism. This individualism could be seen as a refusal to capitulate to the ideological use of love by power: love of fatherland, the good ole USA, the proletariat, the people, whatever. Ideology is more often about hate for the other than about love for them. God is on our side so we can vilify and crush those who oppose who we are, as expressed by our leaders.

We can see an example of the mutual reinforcement of hate between the political and religious in Huckleberry Finn where Huck has grown up with the notion that slaves are property and to help one escape is therefore sinful. Lost, drifting down the waters of a river, this poor white trash has come to form a loving bond with a slave, transgressing the ethical teachings of the day. The apex of the novel is the decision by Huck to defy everything and help a slave escape. Not only will the act make him a criminal for stealing the 'property' of another but it will destine him to hell. After an agonizing decision Huck declares, "All right, then, I'll GO to hell,"[74] in one of the most famous passages in American literature. One has only to read that line to a bunch of young kids and see them pump their fists in the air in approval to understand how inherent our moral sense is before it is twisted by the ethics of hate.

In the end however, Kierkegaard's subservience to the Bible, amounts to something similar to that which he opposes. He claims to be defined by a savagery, equated with paganism, where he is incapable of ethical behaviour without being commanded. (We are back, perhaps, to a lust-love polarity. In *The Seducer's Diary* the narrator is a misogynistic seducer playing an aesthetic game of power; an extremely slanderous act to see this as characteristic of all men.) Ethical behaviour, by definition, is dependent on submission to commandment, which is the same assumption of impotence that underlies the authority of all ideology. As Christopher Hitchens said, "belief in the divine…is the origin of all dictatorship."[75] As with all agape, Christian agape could lead to compassion, empathy and responsibility that are a moral force, but what happens instead, with some Christians, is the development of a smug indifference toward others – advocating hate, racism, militarism, and capital punishment – justified by their belief that they have the moral high ground because of their religion.

In Christian discourse there is a continual reference to certain polarities: eros-agape, selfish-selfless. The love of others is debased in relation to the love of God. Sexuality is something for which the church can offer no alternative. It is a challenge, so it is dismissed as lust and ethically unimportant or, worse, damaging. Christian polarities are tied to efforts by the church to control and are artificial, not reflected in the loves we lead where ethical behaviour begins from the obligation and love between individuals, including erotic love, and extends outward to society at large.

The Christian concept of agape was co-opted from the 'pagan' Greeks, but with a fundamental difference. For Plato, agape begins with erotic love, but this develops into love for the good, beauty and knowledge; i.e. the famous notion of 'platonic love' (non-sexual, and of a higher order). It was Thomas Aquinas who inserted God for the good, the beautiful, and knowledge, as the highest and most worthy ideals of love.

Plato recognized that agape grows from what Kiekegaard calls preferential love, and does not require the commandment of God to do this. But his agape is, of course, in line with his idealism. While it begins with the erotic, it eventually disembodies love. Still, it corresponds to our day day-to-day experience of love in ways that Kierkegaard does not. Love is not something static but shifting and developing. As we get older, the intensity and eroticism of a relationship often develops into something more like friendship. What begins with erotic attraction and fulfillment, often with a heavy dose of self-absorption, grows, as love, into concern for the care and well-being of the other without the requirement of religion.

When pushed, the Christian segregation, that we are selfish without God's command, breaks down. People simultaneously act selfishly and selflessly whether they are Christians or not. A mother of a newborn, for example, will act almost completely selflessly, but while she will gradually assert her own needs the capacity for selflessness does not vanish.

Challenging the idea that ethics can only flow from authority brings us back to Austen's choice in relationships. Meeting the social criteria for a good match versus love. On the one side is marriage as a contractual relationship, subject to control by law, religion, class and so on. On the other side is friendship, unrequited love, courtly love, and romantic love; relationships based on undirected love. It is the latter that demands a personal ethical obligation to the other, and that extends outward, politically, to the broader society.

Not only do eros and personal relationships impact ethics and politics but they challenge power. A depiction of this is found in *Hiroshima, mon amour*, the film by Alain Resnais and Marguerite Duras. During a love affair between a French woman and a Japanese man, the story is told of her secret love affair during the Second World War with a German soldier, the official enemy. He is eventually shot and killed in the square of the French town. As described by Linnell Secomb:

> The young woman exposes the secret of their love by publicly holding him and grieving his death. Prioritising her lover, even in death, she risks and suffers being reviled as a traitor. But it is not just her act that is ethical. The film itself, in staging this scene, is a condemnation of the senselessness of war. It privileges ethical responsibility to individual others over the law of the state and the inhuman distinctions between allies and enemies... Hiroshima, mon amour, however, extends this lesson further, creating a link between erotics and politics. The film opens with a scene of love between the Japanese man and the now older French woman – two bodies entangled, caressing, skin-to-skin...this opening scene suggests that the political is already present even in the erotic. The voluptuous movement of the lovers is not only a relation of bodies but also of histories, communities and tragedies.[76]

David Hume's ethical position was independent of religion, but egalitarian in that ethics is portrayed as innate and an obligation of each of us to all others. Hume presents an alternative philosophical approach to idealism, where ethics is based on the world in which we live, re-embodied in the world we know, and on our capacity to understand and feel sympathy for others. He placed the idea of sympathy at the heart of a non-Christian ethics. Sympathy is not selfish, but an innate quality that allows all of us, though different, to find an ethical commonality. "The voice of nature and experience seems plainly to oppose the selfish theory,"[77] he wrote. Although we do act in self-interest, we can recognize a virtuous act that has nothing to do with us, or even one that actually has negative ramifications for us.

One application of Hume's philosophical approach (combined with Rousseau, so it applies to all of nature) came from Percy Bysshe Shelley, the English Romantic poet. In his essay, *A Defence of Poetry*, Shelley spoke of ethics as that which does not grow out of self-interest but out of the imagination, that part of our nature that goes beyond reason. Rebellion begins by self-transformation.

> The great secret of morals is love; or a going out of our own nature, and an identification of ourselves with the beautiful which exists in thought, action, or person, not our own. A man, to be greatly good, must imagine intensely and comprehensively; he must put himself in the place of another

and of many others; the pains and pleasures of his species must become his own. The great instrument of moral good is the imagination; and poetry administers to the effect by acting upon the cause.[78]

Shelley goes beyond Hume's idea of sympathy. Irving Singer notes that "Shelley not only emphasizes the importance of imagination as a means of overcoming selfishness, but also immediately applies the analysis to understanding the nature of love."[79]

Hume speaks of affections passing from person to person and begetting 'correspondent movements' on the analogy of 'strings equally wound up, the motion of one communicates itself to the rest.' All this recurs in Shelley's poetry and theory but now elaborated into beautiful and infinitely varied images of reverberation, of resonating harmonics within the soul and between the passions, of complex interactions that unite not just human beings but also everything man can recognize as kindred spirit. And once again, it is love – not just sympathy – that becomes the basic category of analysis. In the *Preface to The Revolt of Islam*, Shelley insists that love is 'the sole law which should govern the moral world.'

In his discussion of 'the amorous passion, or love between the sexes,' Hume lists three components: 'the pleasing sensation arising from beauty; the bodily appetite for generation; and a generous kindness or good-will.' Shelley completely accepts Hume's healthy minded belief that normally the three elements cooperate instead of opposing one another.[80]

Shelley radicalizes Hume's position and makes connections between imagination, love, artistic creation (by which sympathy is developed through imaginative activity) and radical change (remember, from the same essay, it is the poet who is "legislator of the world"). As an essentially Platonic idealist, Shelley saw love as a striving for the beautiful and the good.

From noble intentions there are those who take a pedagogical approach to love. We are told we can make the decision to love someone.

Although one can choose an ethics of love as opposed to one of hate, choosing to treat individuals based on an understanding of love, I have reservations about the idea that one can choose to love someone in an erotic or personal way. What makes love subversive is our inability to control it; like a river it will swirl and meander in unexpected directions. If we didn't know this to be true, we wouldn't, for example, distrust the gay man who says he can reprogram himself and control who he loves. We know that people who are compatible don't necessarily fall in love (in contrast to many self-help books which espouse the Platonic idea that we are parts of a half who spend our lives searching for our one and only matching half). It is just this quality of love, that it is a largely uncontrollable expression of our humanity, which makes it an ethical weapon against ideology. Every act of love is a refusal of prejudice and hate regardless of who the person is. It is precisely this which makes the love we feel individually, in a couple or in a group, a radical ethical and political force. It challenges attempts to lead and direct us. "I love you without knowing how, or when, or from where," wrote Pablo Neruda in a sonnet, whose popularity is a testament to the fact that people recognize that the love they feel intensely is not something controlled.

Erich Fromm, one of those who makes the argument that we can decide whom to love, tries to bolster the idea by referring to the declaration to 'love and honour' in the marriage vow. We wouldn't have to swear an oath to love if there was no choice about it, if love wasn't a conscious decision. But this is not really a choice to create love so much as to promise to attend and commit to it. The wedding vow is more in line with the way that Simon Critchley describes a marriage based on love (defining love as those acts which are not selfish). It is a commitment to nurture an existing love (not to create one):

> I have to wind this watch every day, because it constantly stops. If I don't have it on my wrist, it will stop in an hour or so. So the watch only works insofar as I vigorously shake it every day, which makes its mechanism function for another few hours. I think love is like that; love is that act of the constant shaking of oneself. So I think contentment is a selfish obsessional structure into which one slips back, and love is the countermovement to that. It's that shaking up of the subject, which forces it back into the act of committing.[81]

bell hooks is another who takes a pedagogical approach. Her belief that we can choose love is based on her advocacy of an ethics based on love. Embracing such an ethics can be a political decision (and this is undoubtedly significant, heroic and against all odds at times) or it can be a choice made by someone to repudiate their poor behaviour, such as by an abusive parent to their child. But I think in a personal case such as the latter, love is also spoken about as commitment to an existing love and to the ethical behaviour love demands rather than a manufacturing of love. hooks is a significant writer but I think her definition of love as a verb, as a way of acting, is potentially harmful. Child abuse is defined as a lack of love. In describing child abuse in this way a child is being told not that her abusive parent is confused or mistaken, but that her parent abuses her because he or she doesn't love her. I think this is potentially as damaging to the child as the abuse.

The pedagogical approach recognizes that ethical behaviour is a choice we can make, that we can learn about others, that commitment is a choice, that politics is a choice, but this is much different than proof we have power over love or that ethics is not an innate part of being human.

∽

13

IN THE 1970'S, IVAN Illich argued for limits to industrial production, which meant advocating political action (which he referred to as 'socialist').[82] By the 1990's however, in a conversation with (then) former California Governor Jerry Brown, Illich rejected the idea of commencing change via politics. He placed the decline of love and friendship at the centre of his critique. For Illich, the ethical is an outcome of the practice of friendship between individuals, so political change must flow from that. This is a reversal of the Greek conception that political life was primary and established an ethical society in which friendships could flourish.

> Now, friendship in the Greek tradition, in the Roman tradition, in the old tradition, was always viewed as the highest point which virtue can reach. Virtue meaning here the habitual facility of doing the good thing which is fostered by what the Greeks called politaea, political life, community life...They conceived of friendship as a flowering, a supreme flowering of

the interaction which happens in a good political society...But I do not believe that friendship today can flower out, can come out, of political life. I do believe that if there is something like a political life to be, to remain for us, in this world of technology, then it begins with friendship. Therefore my task is to cultivate disciplined, self-denying, careful, tasteful friendships.[83]

Illich emphasized the concept of hospitality. Because of technology, we have lost that face-to-face interaction that friendship requires. It is important to have a physical doorway and threshold (things not present with technology) that we may help the stranger. He wanted to return to the ethics of the Bible. Like Leo Tolstoy, Illich was a Christian anarchist who saw the damages inflicted by institutions. In his view, charity had become institutionalized, which removed the necessity of individual responsibility. This was crippling. The idea of charity had been expanded through hospitals, schools and other public and religious services. Love was administered by others on our behalf.

I have to make my mind up whom I will take into my arms, to whom I will lose myself, whom I will treat as that vis-a-vis that face into which I look which I lovingly touch with my fingering gaze, from whom I accept being who I am as a gift.[84]

The turn-of-the-century German socialist/anarchist Gustav Landauer wrote that: "The state is a social relationship; a certain way of people relating to one another. It can be destroyed by creating new social relationships; i.e. by people relating to one another differently."[85] Like Illich, he saw the building of virtuous relationships as the driver of change. Inevitably this meant that change rested on the individual accepting ethical responsibility. Landauer advocated for social and cultural change rather than political. He envisioned a multitude of small communal actions that together would transform society. They were cellular parts of a whole (which, in theory, would maintain local autonomy and yet enable broader collaboration). His was not an advocacy of class-based revolution, but of change that was inclusive of all, slipping in and around capitalism. All acts of community – a community garden, an alternative school – were significant. It was change in the here and now, and autonomous, not something that was attempting to enact a grand scheme for the future as devised by an authoritarian group or person.

Landauer thought of 'community' in three ways. The first way was of these temporary autonomous groupings, the second way was the forms of community that were historic and created by authority to control people (the sort which love transgresses), and the third was the historical, universal community that the individual is a part of. He spoke of a kind of self-annihilation that was necessary to be a member of mankind (which Simon Critchley has pointed out is similar to Porete's idea of self-annihilation as necessary for a transgressive, mystical union).[86] For Landauer, this was a fundamentally different experience from the love and other abstractions that served authority. (This takes us full circle, back to his idea that social change rests on 'new social relationships,' pointing to the fact that new sorts of temporary community should not become a base of authoritarian behaviour. They should not be allowed to ossify in that direction.)

It is not that thinkers such as Illich and Landauer didn't realize the case for political action, of course they did, but they argued that the first step in activism should be to restructure the relationship between themselves and the state. They chose empowerment and refused to allow political authority to dictate the nature of their relationships and the options for action available to them. They focused on the ethical relationship between people, and to emphasize that future change also reflect this. Attempting to work towards change within an authoritarian structure leads to the same sort of power structure within the movement for change. Political activity proceeding from love is either an affirmation of some authority or, from the beginning, it is transgressive.

Gandhi was an interesting figure in this respect who also felt that love was the central principle of life. His homespun clothes were part of a sort of primitive anarchism that advocated self-sufficient lifestyles where community could grow. The emphasis on love, in seeing it as the central principle of life, generated and reinforced a number of political views from anti-imperialism to a rejection of the typical economic solutions to poverty based on being part of a market economy rather than self-sufficiency. His views contradict those of a revolutionist Left, but I think it is reasonable to argue that he was consistent in thinking that it is hypocritical to try to expand the realm of love with violence.* Gandhi also feared the emphasis on the state by much of the Left and the sup-

---

* Shelley was another who saw pacifism in a political way. "Love was subversion, from the very moment that desire, or magnetic attraction, caused the atoms to swerve defiantly aside. Love was emphatic and, once unshakeably linked to will, not only perturbing but invincible. In Shelley's awakened world it would be followed without question, each man and woman turning outwards from the self to the other, with love flowing like electric current through their clasped, determined hands...He strove to encourage in England the liberation movements that were rising in Naples and Spain and Greece. He imagined another Peterloo, in which the people would stand with folded arms in dauntless defiance of armed soldiers...By gazing on evil in love, they became stronger. They could turn it to good. They would be martyred, but their courage would spur fervent imitation; the slaughter of one crowd would inspire resistance in the next, until a great wave of humanity would surge against injustice." (Wroe, 343.)

position that political change had to happen in order for love and personal relationships to grow. He came from a culture that saw self-enlightenment as the highest of endeavours. He doesn't reverse the desired order of personal change and political change, in the way that Illich did, but advocated that both should happen simultaneously.

Gandhi's notions have a relevancy beyond the 'developing' world. We can see the valorization of shared endeavour among those who participate in a community garden, choose to live in a co-op, play on a house league team, build a house with friends, or play in a band. Illich spoke of friendship as being like a musical chord, and it can be, but an autonomous group is more like the improvisational band that moves together while allowing for individuation. For this type of association to be different than a controlled community it has to be dissolvable, if it begins to ossify into a base of power for some element within it.

There is a revolutionary tradition that sees love as central to their critique and political agenda, and which combines the cultural sphere with the political. It is a tradition that runs from Shelley (the poet is the "legislator of the world") through the Surrealists and culminates in the Situationist International (SI) who spoke of the end of art by its suppression and realization in day-to-day life so that art is no longer a separate activity from living. It recognizes the close connection between love and the imagination, freedom, and the ability to express love.

> The surrealists' exploration of desire was influenced by psychoanalysis but not subservient to it... They also ultimately - and in their poetic texts quite insistently - preferred a vision of desire as an active, ever-creative force, to a concept of desire founded on the notion of lack.[87]

The Surrealists wanted to liberate sexuality and desire but theirs wasn't just a project about expanding sexual freedom (although it was that). The Surrealists did not have the reverential tone of Ansel Adams, but they were like him in seeing the equality between the subjective and objective. Surrealists saw mad and chaotic love as a challenge to the world of rationality. Giving rein to desire, dreams, and passion leads us to want to remake the world on behalf of human freedom; the most extreme act of human creativity that comes when love is granted primacy. As a revolutionary group they hoped to unleash human passions that would create a thirst for revolutionary change. Like the comments of dk, previously quoted, it takes effort to overcome years of indoctrination, to be able to use art to genuinely express love and to honestly interact with others in a spontaneous way.

The Situationist International was significant (like all who focus on love) in seeing daily life as central to their analysis and the measure of change. This puts love and basic humanity at the centre of politics and culture. In *The Revolution of Everyday Life*, one of their most significant tracts, and a book that was widely quoted during the May '68 rebellion in France, Raoul Vaneigem would write:

> Because of its increasing triviality, everyday life has gradually become our central preoccupation…People who talk about revolution and class struggle without referring explicitly to everyday life, without understanding what is subversive about love and what is positive in the refusal of constraints, such people have corpses in their mouths.[88]

Perhaps nowhere is there so provocative and devastating a critique of modern life as that found in the writings of the SI.

In their view, human relationships have become commodity relations. The commodity dominates life and determines how we relate to each other. Objects relating to objects. We are spectators of our own lives, which are mediated by images. The spectacle is the central production of society; this dream world where people are alienated and separate from each other. Our lives are defined by our alienation, boredom and lack of poetry. Architecture and city design enhance the separation between people. Between rapid transit and technology there is no physical contact with those we are close to. We don't even know our neighbours. Nothing short of a complete revolutionary re-shaping of society will allow for authentic relationships and personal control of our lives. Mere survival is not enough. Fragmentary resistance will be recuperated and sold back to us.

I don't think that there is a necessary conflict between this sort of revolutionist view and the activities of those who seek to expand and act on love as individuals, couples or groups. Love is a central part of our basic humanity and our natural resistance to the spectacle, repression and boredom. Those cited above share some essential commonalities. They act on the inner logic of love and take a radical position, refusing to channel their efforts through political and institutional centres of power that can claim to act in the name of love, but destroy autonomous human relationships. There is a recognition too of the significance of human contact and of the creativity of love, and that its exchange is not an economic transaction.

In a recent article in *Le Monde*, French philosopher Edgar Morin, himself a participant in the '68 rebellion, wrote (regarding political ecology) that what has not been assimilated by the Left is Ivan Illich's message from the 1970's. Morin's article proposes that a new solidarity can develop from the Left absorbing Illich's message, which would, in turn, regenerate the political field. "Today's Leftism is now suffering from a revolutionarism deprived of revolution.

It justly denounces the neoliberal economy and capitalism's outbursts, but it is unable to suggest an alternative. The term 'anti-capitalist party' betrays this failing."[89]

> Illich formulated an original criticism of our civilization that showed to what extent material progress entailed psychological unease, how hyper-specialisation in education or medicine produced new forms of blindness and how necessary it was to regenerate what he calls friendly human relations. Whilst the environmental message was slowly seeping into political awareness, the Illichian message remained confined...The calculation applied to all aspects of human life leaves out what cannot be calculated, that is to say, suffering, happiness, joy and love, basically, what is important in our lives and appears extra-social and purely personal. All the solutions that have been considered are quantitative: economic growth, GDP growth. When will politics take into account humankind's huge need for love lost in outer space?...This would make us understand that establishing new types of solidarity is a key aspect of a civilization policy.
> Political ecology should not isolate itself. It can and should take root in liberating political principles that have animated republican, socialist then communist ideologies which have irrigated the civic conscience of Left wing people in France. Thus, political ecology could enter a wide regenerated political field and contribute to regenerating it...The existential path would be a path of life reform, where what is obscurely felt by each person would be part of consciousness, that love and understanding are a human being's most precious goods and that the most important thing is to live poetically, that is to say in one's fulfilment, communion and ardour.[90]

Morin makes the case for a revised political Left, invigorated by love. His argument is based on the necessity of undertaking actions which confront the dangers threatening our existence. In *The Value of Nothing*, Raj Patel, is another who (although he doesn't mention Illich) could be said to be updating the type of approaches that Illich espoused. Patel advocates for the restoration of the commons, and for the reclamation of popular control over resources (including technological) that are now under a corporate control which exploits them and values them only as commodities. While Patel speaks about community control and local initiatives on the one hand, he also sees the restoration of the commons as requiring political action to limit the ability of corporations to control resources.

In the U.S. many conservatives champion fundamentalist Christianity for political ends. (e.g. They have adopted positions on issues like abortion – previously seen as a Catholic issue – after fundamentalists embraced it in order to exploit it politically.[91]) Although claiming to speak for love, conservatives are often the biggest proponents of the politics of hate. They advocate censorship, war, more policing and executions, male dominance, racism, homophobia and the transfer of economic wealth to the rich. They seek power by dangling the false promise of more love in people's lives through a return to a non-existent past where Americans were enmeshed in the love of family, within a loving Christian community (with no 'others' present, except as servants) as directed by God.

It is a sad fact that we have become so inured to the hate that spews from mainstream (particularly conservative) politicians that a US presidential candidate can become a front-runner while talking of a 'gay lifestyle' as Satanic, that 'multiculturalism' (code for Muslim immigration in this context) is attacked by the chancellor of Germany, and the prime minister of Italy makes regular racist comments with impunity. While the background of fascism in these two countries darts in and out of view, hate is not confined to only a few countries nor to these few examples. It is ubiquitous. Conservative governments dominate in the West.

I live in Canada where the prime minister recently said that the biggest threat the country faces is "Islamicism,"[92] and in Toronto, the mayor, with pride, recently announced his opposition to every single type of public assistance that the city offers. He chooses not to think about who the recipients of assistance are or the sort of help they receive. He made his pronouncement so it could be seen that he acts strictly in the name of ideology, an ideology which seeks to eliminate social spending, replacing it with nothing. It is the abdication of all ethical responsibility and a proud proclamation of the absence of thought (and manufacturing stupidity, by attacking science and by other actions, is central to today's conservatism because it relies so heavily on propaganda and the undermining of democracy.)[93] Locally, at the current time, this means increasing money for police while cutting money for libraries. (When local novelist Margaret Atwood spoke out against the latter, the mayor's brother, a member of city council, proudly flaunted his ignorance, proclaiming that he wouldn't "have a clue who she is" if Atwood walked by him.)[94]

This essay was undertaken to argue in the affirmative for love. For good reason, love has been attacked regularly in intellectual discourse for the last century (often focusing on its role in an economically driven world). It is selfish (Sartre), prostitution (Marx), servitude (feminism), a commodity (Slater). Freud and his followers have sought to describe its pathologies.[95]

My argument is that while authority attempts to control love to support itself, love is also our means of challenging that power. Love transgresses authoritarian boundaries regarding race, age, religion, gender, class, politics and ethnicity. It is a fundamentally creative force and a means of resistance to oppression of every sort. It is the basis of an ethics free from institutional control, and demands that we assume ethical responsibility for others. It brings us together and emphasises the importance of happiness in day-to-day life. These are all of critical importance if we are to challenge the politics of hate.

ENDNOTES

1. William Butler Yeats, "When You Are Old," Representative Poetry On-line, http://rpo.library.utoronto.ca/poem/3828.html.
2. Dylan Thomas, "Love In The Asylum," ShadowPoetry.com, http://www.shadowpoetry.com/resources/famous/thomas/dylan.html.
3. Peter Blegvad, "How Beautiful You Are," *The Naked Shakespeare*, CD, Virgin Records.
4. George Orwell, *1984*, George-orwell.org, http://www.george-orwell.org/1984/22.html.
5. Harriet Jacobs, *Incidents in the Life of a Slave Girl*, Pagebypagebooks.com, http://www.pagebypagebooks.com/Harriet_Jacobs/Incidents_in_the_Life_of_a_Slave_Girl/A_Perilous_Passage_In_The_Slave_Girls_Life_p2.html.
6. Jacobs, http://www.pagebypagebooks.com/Harriet_Jacobs/Incidents_in_the_Life_of_a_Slave_Girl/The_Lover_p5.html.
7. bell hooks, *Salvation: Black People and Love* (New York: HarperCollins Publishers Inc., 2001) XXIII.

8. Hooks, XXI, XXIV, 16.
9. Thomas Cahill, *Mysteries of the Middle Ages* (New York: Anchor Books, 2008) 121.
10. Cahill, 128.
11. Referenced in: Wikipedia, "Troubadour," http://en.wikipedia.org/wiki/Troubadour (accessed Feb 21, 2011).
12. Peter Marshall, "William Blake: Revolutionary Romantic" in *Revolutionary Romanticism*, ed. Max Blechman, 53 (San Francisco: City Lights Books, 1999).
13. Marshall, 57.
14. Marshall, 54.
15. Walt Whitman, *Leaves of Grass: The Complete 1855 and 1891-92 Editions* (New York: Library of America Paperback Classics, 2011) 184.
16. Whitman, 249.
17. Whitman, 283.
18. Wikipedia, "Unfinished Music No.1: Two Virgins," http://en.wikipedia.org/wiki/Two_Virgins (accessed May 1, 2011).
19. 20 *Exodus* 12
20. Hillary Mayell, "Thousands of Women Killed for Family 'Honor'," National Geographic.com, http://news.nationalgeographic.com/news/2002/02/0212_020212_honorkilling.html (accessed June 1, 2011).
21. *Romeo and Juliet* V, iii, 300-302.
22. Jane Austen, *Pride and Prejudice* (Oxford: Oxford University Press, 1998) 273-274.
23. Jane Austen, *Sense and Sensibility* (Oxford: Oxford University Press, 1998).
24. Sudhir Kakar, ed. *Indian Love Stories* (New Delhi: Lotus Collection, 1999) 12.
25. Adela Finch, "Introduction," *Emma*, Jane Austen (Oxford: Oxford University Press, 2003) xii.
26. Philip Slater, *The Pursuit of Loneliness* (Boston: Beacon Press, 1990) 80.
27. Erich Fromm, *The Art of Loving* (New York: Harper, 2006) 3.
28. Raoul Vaneigem, *The Revolution of Everyday Life*, trans. Donald Nicholson-Smith (London: Rebel Press, 1981) 27.
29. David Cox, "How 'Never Let Me Go' gave up and died," *The Guardian*, February 14, 2011, http://www.guardian.co.uk/film/filmblog/2011/feb/14/never-let-me-go-fate?intcmp=239 (accessed Mar 1, 2011).
30. Jerry Brown, "Ivan Illich with Jerry Brown," *We The People*, KPFA, Mar 22, 1996, http://www.wtp.org/achive/transcripts/ivan_illich_jerry.html (accessed May 1, 2011).
31. Michael Atkinson "Friend Your Day Away: The Anti-Social Network." *In These Times*, February 2011, http://www.inthesetimes.com/article/6847/friend_your_day_away_the_anti-social_network/ (accessed Mar 1, 2011).
32. Ivan Illich, *Tools For Conviviality* (New York: Harper & Row, 1973), clevercycles.com, http://clevercycles.com/tools_for_conviviality/ (accessed June 1, 2011).
33. Raj Patel, *The Value of Nothing* (Toronto: Harper Collins, 2009) 169.
34. Wikipedia. "Cultural Revolution," http://en.wikipedia.org/wiki/Cultural_Revolution (accessed Mar 1, 2011).
35. Murray Whyte, "Winds of change propel China's new art stars," *The Toronto Star*,

Dec 12, 2009, http://www.thestar.com/unassigned/article/737386—winds-of-change-propel-china-s-new-art-stars (accessed Jan 1, 2011).
36. Laura Kipnis, *Against Love*, (New York, Pantheon Books, 2003) 169.
37. Haughney, Kathleen, "Unmarried? Living together? You're breaking the law in Florida," SunSentinel.com, Aug 31, 2011, http://articles.sun-sentinel.com/2011-08-31/news/fl-adultery-repeal-bill-20110829_1_unmarried-couples-cohabitation-adultery (accessed Sept 1, 2011)
38. Alyce Mahon, *Eroticism and Art* (Oxford: Oxford University Press, 2005) 15.
39. Mahon, 16.
40. Nelson Algren, *Chicago: City on the Make* (Chicago: University of Chicago Press, 1983) 97.
41. Citation in: "Ansel Adams: A Documentary Film," American Experience, PBS.org, http://www.pbs.org/wgbh/amex/ansel/filmmore/pt.html (accessed Feb 1, 2011).
42. Paolo Nutini, "Coming Up Easy," *Sunny Side Up*, CD, Atlantic.
43. Citation in: Wikipedia. "Muse," http://en.wikipedia.org/wiki/Muse (accessed Mar 1, 2011).
44. Robert McLiam Wilson, *Eureka Street* (London: Vintage, 1998) 1.
45. Irving Singer, *Philosophy of Love: A Partial Summing Up* (Cambridge: The MIT Press, 2009) 36.
46. Cornelius Cardew, *Treatise Handbook* (London: Peters Edition, 1971).
47. Emily Dickinson, *The Complete Poems of Emily Dickinson* (Boston: Little, Brown and Company, 1960) 114.
48. "Shelley," *The Cambridge History of English and American Literature*, Volume XII, The Romantic Revival, Ward & Trent, et al (New York: G.P. Putnam's Sons, 1907–21) Bartleby.com, http://www.bartleby.com/222/0307.html (accessed Mar 1, 2011).
49. Percy Byshhe Shelley, "Epipsychidion," Department of Electrical and Computer Engineering. University of Puerto Rico Mayagüez, http://ece.uprm.edu/artssciences/ingles/nb-epipsychidion.htm (accessed Apr 1, 2011).
50. Ann Wroe, *Being Shelley: The Poet's Search For Himself* (New York: Pantheon Books, 2007) 367.
51. Dickinson, Emily, *The Complete Poems of Emily Dickinson* (Boston: Little, Brown and Company, 1960) 262.
52. Nancy Dzaja, "Lovesickness: The Most Common Form of Heart Disease," University of Western Ontario Medical Students, http://www.uwomeds.com/uwomj/V78n1/Lovesickness.pdf (accessed Apr 1, 2011).
53. Forough Farrokhzad, "Conquest of the Garden," ForughFarrokhzad.org, http://www.forughfarrokhzad.org/selectedworks/selectedworks4.asp (accessed Apr 1, 2011).
54. Farrokhzad. "It Is Only Sound That Remains," http://www.forughfarrokhzad.org/selectedworks/selectedworks6.asp (accessed Apr 1, 2011).
55. Sayd Bahodine Majrouh, *Songs of Love and War: Afghan Women's Poetry* (New York: Other Press, 2010) 2.
56. Majrouh. 26, 76, 55, 9, 53, 64.

57. Majrouh, 56.
58. St Teresa d'Avila, *The Life of Teresa of Jesus* (1515–1582), citation in Wikipedia, "Ecstasy of Saint Theresa," http://en.wikipedia.org/wiki/Ecstasy_of_Saint_Theresa (accessed May 1, 2011).
59. Ellen L. Babinsky, "Preface," *The Mirror of Simple Souls* (New York: Paulist Press, 1993) 2.
60. Simon Critchley, *How to Stop Living and Start Worrying* (Cambridge: Polity Press, 2010) 63.
61. Babinsky, 40.
62. Critchley, 64-65.
63. Susan Davis, "Eros Meets Civilization: Gershon Legman Confronts The Post Office," *Serpents In The Garden*, eds. Alexander Cockburn and Jeffrey St. Clair (Petrolia: Counterpunch, 2004) 257.
64. Jordan Flaherty, "Criminalizing Consensual Sex," Counterpunch.org. Mar 18-20, 2011, http://www.counterpunch.org/flaherty03182011.html (accessed Apr 1, 2011).
65. Hans Christian Anderson, "The Little Mermaid," Gilead.org, http://hca.gilead.org.il/li_merma.html (accessed Feb 1, 2011).
66. Greg Thompson, "Angel Day Turning." Google Video, http://video.google.ca/videoplay?docid=4755533137197872737# (accessed Apr 1, 2011).
67. Simone De Beauvoir, *Memoirs of a Dutiful Daughter* (New York: Harper Collins, 1959).
68. *Surrealist Love Poems*, ed. Mary Ann Caws (Chicago: University of Chicago Press, 2001).
69. Fromm, 24.
70. Citation in: Vaneigem, 29.
71. Whitman, Walt, "Calamus poems: from *Leaves of Grass* (1860), Electronic Text Center, University of Virginia Library, http://etext.virginia.edu/etcbin/toccer-new2?id=WhiCala.sgm&images=images/modeng&data=/texts/english/modeng/parsed&tag=public&part=39&division=div1 (accessed May 1, 2011).
72. John D. Caputo, *How To Read Kierkegaard* (London: Granta Books, 2007) 96.
73. Caputo, 97.
74. Mark Twain, *The Adventures of Huckleberry Finn* (New York: Random House, 1996) 273.
75. Richard Lea, "Christopher Hitchens jokes about joining 'cancer elite,'" Guardian Online, Mar 7, 2011, http://www.guardian.co.uk/books/2011/mar/07/christopher-hitchens-jokes-about-cancer (accessed Apr 1, 2011).
76. Linnell Secomb, *Philosophy and Love: From Plato to Popular Culture* (Indiana: Indiana University Press, 2007) 66.
77. David Hume, *An Enquiry Concerning the Principles of Morals*, Philosophy Index, Apr 1, 2011, http://philosophy-index.com/hume/principals-morals/v.php (accessed May 1, 2011).
78. Percy Bysshe Shelley, "A Defence of Poetry," Bartleby.com, http://www.bartleby.com/27/23.html (accessed May 1, 2011).

79. Irving Singer, *The Nature of Love Vol. 2, Courtly and Romantic* (Chicago: The University of Chicago Press, 1984) 424.
80. Singer, 424-5.
81. Critchley, 72.
82. Illich, 1973.
83. Brown.
84. Brown.
85. Gustav Landauer, *Revolution and Other Writings: A Political Reader* (Oakland: PM Press, 2010) 3.
86. Critchley, 67.
87. *Surrealism: Desire Unbounded*, ed. Jennifer Mundy (Princeton: Princeton University Press, 2001).
88. Vaneigem, 9, 15.
89. Edgar Morin, "Changing man's relationship to nature is only a start," Goodplanet.info, Mar 1, 2011, http://www.goodplanet.info/eng/Contenu/Points-de-vues/Changing-man-s-relationship-to-nature-is-only-a-start/(theme)/1405 (accessed Apr 1, 2011).
90. Morin.
91. Sarah Moughty, "Meet The Christian Philosopher Who Shaped Michele Bachmann's Views," Frontline, August 10, 2011, http://www.pbs.org/wgbh/pages/frontline/government-elections-politics/meet-the-christian-philosopher/ (accessed Sept. 1, 2011).
92. Jane Taber, "Harper's 'Islamicism' remark draws heavy opposition fire," GolbeandMail.com, Sept 7, 2011, http://www.theglobeandmail.com/news/politics/ottawa-notebook/harpers-islamicism-quip-draws-heavy-opposition-fire/article2156458/ (accessed Sept. 7, 2011)
93. Mark Howard, "Study Confirms That Fox News Makes You Stupid," alternet.org, Dec. 15, 2010, http://www.alternet.org/story/149193/study_confirms_that_fox_news_makes_you_stupid (accessed Sept. 7, 2011)
94. Elizabeth Church, "Library cuts will happen 'in a heartbeat,' Doug Ford says," globeandmail.com, Jul. 26, 2011, http://www.theglobeandmail.com/news/national/toronto/library-cuts-will-happen-in-a-heartbeat-doug-ford-says/article2110242/ (accessed Sept. 7, 2011)
95. Robert C. Solomon and Kathleen M. Higgins, "Introduction", *The Philosophy of (Erotic) Love*, eds. Robert C. Solomon and Kathleen M. Higgins (Lawrence: University Press of Kansas, 1991) 7-8.

Images

Cover.	Egon Schiele, *Untitled*, Location Unknown.
Frontispiece.	Egon Schiele, *Girlfriends*, Private Collection.
Page 7.	Ernst Barlach, *Illustration for Goethe's "Walpurgisnacht,"* North Carolina Museum of Art, Raleigh.
Page 11.	Thomas E. Askew, *Portrait*, Private Collection.
Page 15.	Dante Gabriel Rossetti, *Study for the Dancing Girls for "The Bower Meadow,"* Birmingham Art Gallery, Birmingham.
Page 23.	Wilhelm Oesterle, *Untitled*, Los Angeles County Museum of Art, Los Angeles.
Page 27.	Dorothea Maetzel-Johanssen, *Mutter und Kind*, Los Angeles County Museum of Art, Los Angeles.
Page 31.	*Children Playing Outdoors, Eatonville, Florida*, Lomax Collection, Library of Congress, Washington.
Page 35.	Json/brokenchopstick, *Watching The Show*, Wikimedia Commons. Flickr_DSC8137.
Page 39.	Maude (Lennox) Dube, Courtesy of R. Dubey.
Page 43.	Elizabeth Siddal, *Lovers Listening to Music*, Ashmolean Museum, Oxford.
Page 49.	Suzanne Valadon, *Femmes et enfant au bord de l'eau*, Portland Art Museum, Portland.
Page 61.	Christian Rohlfs, *Zwei Tanzenda*, Davis Museum and Cultural Center, Wellesley, MA.
Page 65.	Maude (Lennox) Dube, Courtesy of R. Dubey.
Page 73.	Ernst Ludwig Kirchner, *Fränzi Fehrmann und Peter*, Kirchner Museum, Davos.
Page 81.	Richard Throssel, *Crow Girls With Dogs*, American Heritage Center, University of Wyoming, Laramie.

ALSO FROM
CHARIVARI PRESS

SCARLET LETTER #1

INDECENT ACTS IN A PUBLIC PLACE: SPORTS, INSOLENCE & SEDITION
by Rod Dubey
$10.95

Indecent Acts In A Public Place offers four provocative essays that mark a radical departure from traditional descriptions of sports as a cultural event. It rejects any notion that sport is merely a passive consumer activity that indoctrinates the participant into particular social values and acceptance of his representation. Instead, these essays look at challenges by sports fans and athletes to the cathartic spectacle and their own seeming impotence. They argue that what is absolutely essential to sport, and what makes sport so popular, are its qualities of contestation of external authority and representation, hedonism and possibilities for creativity. For it is just these qualities (noise, disruption, festival, sensuality and antisocialness) that sport, as a business, seeks both to contain and commodify.

Indecent Acts In A Public Place considers sport with an attention to current critical theory that is usually reserved for 'high art,' yet at the same time it is accessible, polemical, imaginative and witty. Along the way it takes up such fascinating and amusing questions as "Why do baseball players spit?" and "Why are athletes usually stupid?"

He suggests, that the game itself, along with other sports (such as baseball) at first banned by the Church and state because of their threat to 'order', were then organized, controlled (with their own laws) and contained on pitches and eventually in stadiums, before finally as is the case in the current era, appropriated as 'spectacle' within the Global media network. This, at the same time as further disenfranchising those playing the unsanctioned game on the terraces: 'Not surprisingly, a working class youth often sees soccer hooliganism as an initial means of effecting change ...' (Rod Dubey)"

—Doug Aubrey, *Variant.*

Also From

CHARIVARI PRESS

Music IS Rapid Transportation
...from the Beatles to Xenakis

Editor: Daniel Kernohan

$21.95

by Lawrence Joseph, Dan Lander, Donal McGraith, Bill Smith,
Alan Stanbridge, Scott Thomson & Vern Weber

photos by Gordon Bowbrick, Herb Greenslade & Bill Smith

A truly alternative look at music lists, not one that merely includes the obvious but shows the connections of popular music to the avant garde, the obscure, the experimental, the quirky, and the adventurous. Herein you will find a list of 500 artists from the familiar to the unknown. A list and a guide to musical pleasure sometimes close at hand and sometimes far afield. The book includes biographical essays of the eight contributors describing their musical journeys of discovery and the joy they derived from that exploration. They discuss the merits and dilemmas of collecting, recording versus live performance, the change of media and the future of music. In addition 100 plus artists receive short and detailed personal evaluation.

These essays are often very personal and the contributors provide contexts (mostly cultural and occassionally personal and political) for their developments and discoveries. There's very little journalistic detachment here and that's a good thing. ... Each writer in his own way conveys the elation, that zing, of discovering and relishing new sounds. Any eclectic music geek will identify with these stories. ... When music heads bemoan the amount of crappy music out there that clogs our plane of existence, they fail to remember just how much good stuff is out there waiting to be discovered. Music IS Rapid Transportation is more than just a reminder; it may prove to be indispensable to tommorrow's musical Magellans starting out on their own Paths of Discovery.

— Mark Keresman, *Signal to Noise*

ALSO FROM

CHARIVARI PRESS

RANT & DAWDLE
THE FICTIONAL MEMOIR OF COLSTON WILMOTT

AS IMAGINED BY
WILIAM E. SMITH

$28.95

Rant & Dawdle is a fictional memoir comprising thirty-eight interwoven stories from the perspective of a grumpy old man living on a small island off the west coast of Canada and an expectant young boy born into the poverty of WW2 English working class. The old man dreaming in retrospect, the young boy living a developing history, both to eventually rendezvous in the eighties. Filled with the humour and history of a post war generation nurtured on comic books, the Goon Show and jazz.

It's bleedin' brilliant. It's not a book, it's an achievement. Bravo.
    Art Lange - Writer, Producer, Former editor *Downbeat Magazine* (Chicago, USA)

Fantastic! I started reading and found it was almost impossible to stop! What is so great is that I can relate to a lot of things you write about. Thank you very much. And what a brilliant edition!
    Leo Feigen - Leo Records (Newton Abbott, UK)

There is nothing straightforward about Bill Smith's life and career and his rambling, chaotic memoir is no different. ... The life recorded here has been spent in extremes, driven by an obsession with jazz, and fuelled by an irrepressible imagination. ... This is such a hilarious, poignant, and thoroughly captivating tale that ... better to preserve the rough edges than risk toning down and smoothing out the singularly authentic voice so brilliantly captured here.
    —Pamela Margles, *Whole Note Magazine.*

You covered an enormous territory and gave new life to an era of history and ideals that we all need to remember. There were so many things that rang a bell, I wished I'd taken notes. And so many times I laughed!
    Renee Rodin - Writer, Visual Artist, and Cultural Worker (Vancouver, Canada)

ALSO FROM

CHARIVARI PRESS

THAT RECOIL OF NATURE

A NOVEL BY CRAIG GRIMES

$12.95

In 1598 a young Italian noblewoman named Beatrice Cenci murdered her abusive, rapist father. Her actions found many defenders but not the Romantic poet and pacifist Percy Bysshe Shelley, who, in his verse play The Cenci, condemned Beatrice's violent response.

The Romantics encapsulated the counter-culture of the Vietnam War era, but it was Shelley, in particular, who influenced the views of a young hippie, Lawrence MacQuigau, not only about pacifism and Beatrice Cenci, but about free love, atheism, and vegetarianism.

But Lawrence's convictions will soon be put to the test when he reads the journal of his recently deceased mother about a time, immediately after WWII when she was the only doctor in a small isolated town and sought to help a badly abused young woman after the church, the law and the town turned their back on her. The decisions his mother made are about to intrude into Lawrence's life and threaten his young family, forcing him to act.

That Recoil of Nature is a suspenseful novel that tells two stories of survival, and of the linkages between politics and gender politics. It explores the contagion and ethics of violence in the face of power under the shadow of two very different wars; and of people shaped by these experiences. There are no stock characters here. Their actions are complex and sometimes contradictory, and violence, we see, is something all of us are capable of.

Forthcoming From
CHARIVARI PRESS

☙❧

No Viable Option

by Craig Grimes

Spring-Summer 2012

❧

Sound By Artists

Edited by Dan Lander & Micah Lexier

Available Again Fall 2012

❧

The Wild and the Free
Shane: Integrity vs. Loyalty

by Donal McGraith

Fall 2012

☙❧

www.ingramcontent.com/pod-product-compliance
Lightning Source LLC
Chambersburg PA
CBHW021119080526
44587CB00010B/567